LEAVE NO TRACE
in the Outdoors

The Leave No Trace Center for Outdoor Ethics

The member-driven Leave No Trace Center for Outdoor Ethics teaches people of all ages how to enjoy the outdoors responsibly and is the most widely accepted outdoor ethics program used on public lands. Through relevant and targeted education, research, and outreach, the Center ensures the long-term health of our natural world. In its simplest form, Leave No Trace is about making good decisions to protect the world around you—the world we all enjoy. Do your part to pass our nation's heritage of outdoor recreation to future generations by joining us.

Leave No Trace Center for Outdoor Ethics
P.O. Box 997
Boulder, CO 80306
Phone: 800.332.4100
Website: www.LNT.org

The information in this book was created in collaboration with USDI National Park Service, Bureau of Land Management, Fish & Wildlife Service, U.S. Geological Survey, and the USDA Forest Service.

LEAVE NO TRACE
in the Outdoors

Jeffrey L. Marion, PhD

STACKPOLE
BOOKS

Copyright ©2014 by the Leave No Trace Center for Outdoor Ethics

Published by
STACKPOLE BOOKS
5067 Ritter Road
Mechanicsburg, PA 17055
www.stackpolebooks.com

Printed in the United States of America

10 9 8 7 6 5 4 3 2 1

FIRST EDITION

Cover design by Wendy Reynolds
Cover photo by Ben Lawhon

This book is printed by an FSC® certified printer. The Forest Stewardship Council™ encourages responsible management of the world's forests.

Library of Congress Cataloging-in-Publication Data

Marion, Jeffrey L. (Jeffrey Lawrence)
  Leave no trace in the outdoors / Jeffrey L. Marion, PhD.
      pages cm
  Includes bibliographical references and index.
  ISBN 978-0-8117-1363-4
  1. Low-impact camping. 2. Camping—Environmental aspects. 3. Outdoor recreation—Environmental aspects. 4. Hiking—Environmental aspects. I. Title.
  GV198.93.M37 2014
  796.54—dc23
                                    2014005438

Contents

Preface

America's parks, forests, and wildlife refuges preserve some of the most spectacular scenery and pristine natural environments in the world. The U.S. National Parks enjoy an international reputation as "America's best idea," and our legacy and professionalism in managing public lands have served as a role model to protected area managers everywhere. However, our public lands are not without significant threats, including external threats like air pollution, and internal threats like excessive visitation and livestock grazing. Recreational use of public and private lands can negatively affect the places we visit, the animals we observe, and the experiences of other visitors. Native vegetation is trampled, soil is eroded, animals are disturbed, and visitors experience crowding or conflicts with others. While the impacts of a single visitor may be inconsequential, consider the aggregate impacts associated with more than 930 million visitors reported by the federal land management agencies in recent years. Alternatively, consider the impacts from even greater numbers of visitors to state, county, and city parks; forests; and open spaces closer to our homes.

In response to concerns regarding visitor impacts, the national Leave No Trace program was created in 1994 by the federal land management agencies and the National Outdoor Leadership School to develop and promote low-impact outdoor skills and ethics. This program is guided by the Leave No Trace Center for Outdoor Ethics, an educational nonprofit organization dedicated to the responsible enjoyment and active stewardship of the outdoors by all people, worldwide. The Center achieves its mission through education, research, partnerships, and volunteerism. The Center:

+ believes that education is the best means to protect natural lands from recreational impacts while helping maintain access for recreation and enjoyment;
+ is founded on outdoor ethics, whereby a sense of stewardship is gained through understanding and connecting with the natural world;
+ is science based and builds ethical, pragmatic approaches to resource protection for varying types of outdoor recreation and enjoyment;
+ strives to build key partnerships that support education programs, training and communities of volunteers, educators, land managers, organizations, and corporations committed to teaching and instilling the values of Leave No Trace.

Leave No Trace has expanded to become the most fully developed and widely used educational program for teaching low-impact ethics and practices for nonmotorized outdoor pursuits in the United States and in many other countries around the world. Leave No Trace practices have been fully adopted by the federal land management agencies and are commonly communicated by state and local public land managers, the outdoor recreation industry, and many private organizations such as the Boy Scouts, Girl Scouts, and the American Camp Association.

Leave No Trace information is organized around seven core principles designed to communicate the best available low-impact guidance. These practices can be applied anywhere—from remote wilderness or backcountry to local parks or your backyard—and in any recreational endeavor. Leave No Trace principles and practices extend common courtesy and hospitality to other outdoor visitors and to the natural world of which we are all a part. They are based on an abiding respect for nature. This respect, coupled with good judgment and awareness, will allow you to apply the principles to your own unique circumstances. Act on behalf of your love for the places and wildlife that inspire you. Begin by educating yourself and adopting the skills and ethics that enable you to Leave No Trace; then teach others!

For more information about the national Leave No Trace program's educational resources and courses, visit www.LNT.org.

Introduction

> "The land ethic simply enlarges the boundaries of the community to include soils, waters, plants, and animals, or collectively: the land.... In short, a land ethic changes the role of *Homo sapiens* from conqueror of the land-community to plain member and citizen of it. It implies respect for his fellow-members, and also respect for the community as such."
> —Aldo Leopold

Senator Gaylord Nelson founded Earth Day in 1970 to inspire awareness and appreciation for the Earth's natural environment. The oft-repeated question "Are we loving our parks to death?" reveals that even lands set aside for special protection are increasingly subject to the unintentional impacts of outdoor recreation. Every year, millions of outdoor enthusiasts venture out of their homes to walk their dogs, hike along creeks, run on trails, cycle along greenways, fish local ponds, paddle down rivers, and picnic. Our motives vary, but many seek to reconnect with nature, get exercise, view scenery, and see wildlife. However, while our experiences are personally satisfying, they can be costly to the places we visit and the wildlife we observe. Nature can be fragile—our visits sometimes disrupt the environment, even when we aren't aware of it.

Aldo Leopold, in *A Sand County Almanac*, recognized that "a thing is right when it tends to preserve the integrity, stability, and beauty of the biotic community. It is wrong when it tends otherwise." Each of us can do the "right thing" if we accept a personal responsibility to learn about and adopt Leave No Trace outdoor ethics and practices. Make a personal

Whether close to home or in deep wilderness, practicing Leave No Trace is the best way to ensure long-term protection of our shared lands enjoyed for recreation. BEN LAWHON

commitment to avoid or minimize the associated impacts of your outdoor visits—to both our resources and the experiences of other visitors—by making a few simple changes in how you enjoy the outdoors.

Leave No Trace Expands to Meet Frontcountry Needs

Leave No Trace is a code of conduct promoting stewardship practices necessary to protect the ecological and experiential health of outdoor environments. With its historic roots in wilderness and backcountry settings, this national educational program has expanded to include accessible frontcountry environments. Frontcountry includes outdoor areas that are easily accessible by vehicle and mostly visited by day users, such as protected areas close to home and the developed portions of large parks and forests. Common examples of frontcountry activities include walking on trails near home, visits to local or state parks, car camping in developed campgrounds, and large group events like your organization's picnic, club hike, church group outing, or Scout camporee. Almost 90 percent of outdoor recreation activities and visitation occurs in these highly accessible natural settings, so the Leave No Trace Center for Outdoor Ethics has collaborated with public land managers and other organizations to expand its educational efforts to include these areas. Frontcountry practices may differ from those applied in more remote settings, primarily because of site developments and facilities and differences in recreation activities and equipment. This book was developed to provide a comprehensive review of Leave No Trace practices applicable to frontcountry, backcountry, and wilderness environments. Clear rationales and implications from research are also included to provide more compelling reasons for outdoor visitors to adopt recommended low-impact practices. A "Further Reading" section is included on page 103 for those who want to discover more, particularly about the science supporting these practices.

Leave No Trace practices apply to a wide range of outdoor activities, including both daytime and overnight activities occurring on public or private lands. Frontcountry settings often receive intensive visitation and unique types of use that require different low-impact practices than backcountry activities and settings. Examples include large group picnics and camping, dog walking and pet wastes, trespass on private lands, and the introduction and dispersal of non-native species. Experiential impacts, such as crowding and conflicts with other visitors, can be more prevalent

Though the roots of Leave No Trace are in backcountry and wilderness, the skills and ethics are just as important in frontcountry since nearly 90 percent of all outdoor recreation occurs in these areas. BEN LAWHON

in the frontcountry. Backcountry and wilderness settings may be more remote but are nonetheless popular destinations that sometimes accommodate intensive visitation with few to no facilities. As visitation continues to increase, we must learn how to maintain the integrity and character of the outdoors for all living things. Take the responsibility to improve *your* low-impact knowledge, and share it with others to avoid or reduce impacts during your outings.

Leave No Trace practices and ethics are built around seven core principles, but remember that Leave No Trace is *not* about a fixed set of rules. Rather, it is about your awareness of recreational impacts to the environment and the experiences of other visitors and about developing your knowledge of practices to avoid or minimize those impacts. As your outdoor experience and environmental awareness grow, so will your respect for the environment and your concern for its protection. Leave No Trace is about an outdoor ethic that instills personal values that will compel you to care for the outdoor environments that you visit and behave in a way that protects them and the experiential qualities they provide. Leave No Trace principles and practices become particularly important when you consider the combined effects of all outdoor visitors. One poorly located campsite or campfire may have little significance, but millions of such instances seriously degrade the outdoor experience for all. Leaving No Trace is *everyone's* responsibility.

Leave No Trace Skills & Ethics Information

To obtain additional Leave No Trace educational resources, or for information on courses and training, visit the Leave No Trace website at www.LNT.org, or call 1-800-332-4100. Also, see the "Further Reading" section at the end of this book (page 103). More specific information about Leave No Trace practices can be found in a series of more than fifteen booklets that address a diverse array of environments (e.g., Northeast Mountains, Rocky Mountains, Deserts & Canyons) and recreational activities (e.g., Horse Use, Caving, Sea Kayaking). See www.LNT.org for a complete list.

PRINCIPLES OF LEAVE NO TRACE

Plan Ahead and Prepare

Successful outings require good planning and preparation. Every outdoor visit is enhanced when we take time to improve our outdoor knowledge and skills, learn about the area we will visit, carefully plan our trip, and bring the right equipment.

Improve Your Outdoor Knowledge and Skills

Your outdoor knowledge and skills are important elements of safe and enjoyable outdoor visits, whether hiking a woodland trail, bird watching in a local park, or canoeing a whitewater river. Do you and your group members have the knowledge and skills necessary to ensure that you will have a successful and low-impact outing? For example, hiking and camping skills vary by environmental setting, activity, and season. Work to improve your knowledge, or invite others with the necessary abilities on your trip. Seek out opportunities to expand your outdoor knowledge and skills, and convey what you learn to your family, friends, and group members. Remember, poor preparation and knowledge can transform an easy hike into a dangerous situation that threatens the safety of your group. Makeshift campsites, poorly sited campfires, or emergency rescue operations can also impact your surroundings.

Build Leave No Trace into your trip planning. Begin by reading this book and sharing low-impact practices with those who accompany you on outings. Consider taking a Leave No Trace Trainer or Master Educator course (see Courses, p. 91). Learn more about Leave No Trace educational resources and courses at www.LNT.org. Leave No Trace is about

9

Familiarizing yourself with the areas you intend to visit is one of the best ways to ensure that you can minimize your impact. Trailhead kiosks usually offer detailed information on special concerns, rules, and regulations. ALLISON BOZEMAN

selecting the best available low-impact practice based on your knowledge of possible impacts. Developing this knowledge improves your ability to avoid or minimize the impacts of your outdoor visit.

Learn about the Area You Will Visit

Know before You Go. Some settings may be unfamiliar to outdoor enthusiasts, and both private landowners and public land managers have practices they expect you to learn and apply. Examples include common courtesies like leaving fence gates as you find them or regulations such as keeping your dogs on a leash or parking only in designated spots. Seek out and ask landowners or managers about such practices and rules, and be sure everyone in your group knows and abides by them. Doing so can preserve access to these areas and lessen the need for rules and regulations. Most areas used by the public for recreation have websites where you can find relevant guidance—use the information in planning your

Knowing how to use a map and compass is an essential outdoor skill. Plan your route to meet the expectations and skill level of your group. JEFFREY MARION

visit and provide electronic links or copies in your e-mails to friends or group members. Decide what type of area you'd like to visit, and then learn about it in advance—knowing what type of area best meets your needs and researching it thoroughly will save time during your visit.

For public lands be sure to find and carefully read all applicable rules, but also look for tips and recommended practices. Be aware that such rules and practices can vary substantially between and even within protected areas. For example, campfires may be permissible, discouraged, or prohibited depending on location or seasonal fire danger. Similarly, some areas only *recommend* maximum group sizes while others impose strict limits. If you cannot find guidance through Internet searches, call or stop at agency visitor centers to obtain the applicable guidance. It is best to do this in advance of your visit so you can plan your trip accordingly. Here are some topics of special concern to guide your inquiries:

✦ Driving maps/directions

✦ Detailed topographic maps with trails, water sources, and campsites
✦ Regulations applicable to your activity and location
✦ Recommended outdoor practices, including Leave No Trace techniques
✦ Policies related to camping, campfires, pets, groups, fishing, wildlife, and food and trash storage
✦ Natural history information about flora, fauna, or historic and cultural features
✦ Information on area-specific hazards
✦ Emergency contact information

Carefully Plan Your Trip

The most successful outdoor adventures nearly always involve careful pre-trip planning. Even day hiking requires directions, a map and compass, appropriate footwear and clothing, food and water, and knowledge of trail distances and hiking difficulty. Anticipate problems and prepare for them, like unforeseen changes in weather, a twisted ankle, poorly marked trails, lack of restroom facilities, or a flooded stream crossing. Prepare for extreme weather, hazards, and emergencies, and carry a personal locator beacon and/or cell phone with charged batteries (be aware that cell phone service is unreliable in many backcountry areas). Develop contingency plans if your schedule is altered by unexpected events and carry emergency contact information for the local area (e.g., sheriff, land management agency, and local search and rescue) and for your group members (e.g., parent, guardian, or closest relative). Leave a copy of your itinerary and schedule with a trusted friend or family member.

Minimize impacts to resources and other visitors by teaching Leave No Trace practices to group members and ensuring adequate guidance. Be sensitive to the resource impacts associated with your visit and how your group's activities affect the other visitors you encounter.

"Green" Transportation. When planning the logistics of your trip consider public transportation alternatives, including trains or buses, and plan to use the public bus systems available in many National Parks. Search online for transportation options and schedules. If you are driving and visiting with a group, minimize the number of vehicles by carpooling. This helps to diminish congestion and demand on parking spaces in popular parks and forests.

Scheduling Your Trip. Avoid crowding problems by scheduling your trip to avoid times of high use. Doing so can reduce visitor crowding and conflict and impacts like trail widening and the creation or expansion of recreation sites and campsites. You will also ensure more solitude for you and your companions. Locating a parking spot or campsite is always easier during weekday visits or by avoiding holiday and peak weekends. Expect noise and commotion around busy picnic areas, large campgrounds, and developed recreation sites, particularly during times of high use. If you must visit a popular area during a period of higher use, you will encounter less crowded conditions if you avoid or quickly pass through areas with attraction features such as waterfalls or scenic vistas.

Finding an open campsite that is the right size for your group can be especially challenging during times of high visitation, especially near attraction features. Arrive with extra water containers and you can avoid crowds by camping at a less used site away from water sources. Check with local land management agencies for guidance on selecting routes and campsites that can best accommodate your group's needs, and inquire if camping permits are needed. Some areas have use quotas that fill up six months in advance!

Avoid impacts to sensitive resources by scheduling your visit around times or areas where recreation impacts are more likely to occur. Examples include times where frequent rains or snowmelt create muddy trail conditions, or times and areas where wildlife may be nesting or raising young. If you must visit during such times, ask managers to direct you to the most durable trails and least sensitive areas.

Stick to Established Trails and Campsites. Unless you are experienced in low-impact off-trail travel, stick to areas with formal or well-established trails and campsites. Concentrating your activities in these more developed areas prevents harming less-visited pristine areas that require more advanced low-impact skills. If your adventure will be taking you away from roads, visit in small groups when possible and include enough experienced leaders so you can divide your group to travel and camp separately. Large groups can substantially increase the sizes of campsites, which rarely recover because subsequent campers continue using the newly expanded areas. Research shows that new impacts occur quickly, while recovery requires many years or decades. The guidance presented later in this book will help you to avoid such impacts. Remember, we're all trying to share a finite resource.

Bring The Right Gear

"Ten Essentials" of Gear. There are many versions of the "Ten Essentials" list, but most agree that there are certain necessities that every enthusiast should carry when venturing outdoors. Having the right gear is essential to safe and enjoyable trips *and* to minimizing the impacts of your outdoor experience. The type of equipment you'll need will vary depending on your activity and environment, but reviewing the "Ten Essentials" is always a good starting point. Follow that up with consideration of the "Leave No Trace Essentials" to help you avoid or minimize resource and social impacts.

TEN ESSENTIALS

1. Map & compass, GPS
2. Flashlight
3. Extra food
4. Water/purification
5. Extra clothing
6. Rain gear
7. Matches/fire starter
8. Sun protection
9. Pocket knife
10. First-aid kit

The "Leave No Trace Essentials." Wear appropriate shoes so you can stay on and avoid widening muddy trails. Bring a trash bag and pack out all trash, both yours and that of others. Protect wildlife from obtaining human food by bringing containers or gear to store food and trash safely and a screen to strain food particles from dishwater. If you use trekking

Plan ahead to bring some low-impact gear. A small scrubbing pad makes quick work of dirty dishes. Use a piece of fiberglass screen to filter your dishwater. Consider a camp stove for cooking and a candle lantern in place of an evening campfire. Bring a lightweight trowel to dig cat-holes to bury human waste.
JEFFREY MARION

poles, try using them with rubber tips; they cause less damage to plants, soil, and rocks than metal tips. Even walking your dog requires advance planning—bring a leash and plastic bags to clean up your pet's waste.

"Trash-free" Outings. Planning a picnic or campout? Challenge your group with the goal of making it a "trash-free" or "zero-waste" event by opting for reusable containers and utensils to bring and consume all food and drink. If reusable containers are not an option, bring containers you can return home for recycling. Repackage your food to minimize weight, bulk, and trash, and carefully plan your food portions to avoid carrying out leftovers. Reuse food containers and Ziploc bags to store your trash or leftover food. Conduct a trash assessment after the event to help you improve for future events. Try these practices and you'll be amazed at how easily you can avoid creating trash that becomes an expensive burden for land managers to collect and dispose. Trash is also difficult to store safely from wildlife and can be harmful when they consume it. Improperly stored trash can also create nuisance behaviors in otherwise wild animals. Animals that obtain human food and trash often threaten visitor safety and sometimes must be trapped and relocated, or even killed.

Finally, consider low-impact options for cleaning dishes and disposing of cooking oils, food scraps, and dishwater. Use biodegradable soap and bring a kitchen strainer or piece of fiberglass screen to filter food particles from graywater (cooking or dishwater), and a container to carry home used cooking oil or bacon grease. If you're camping in a developed campground, check with the hosts or rangers for proper graywater disposal practices and bring a container to carry it to a sink or sump. For vehicle-assisted activities, it may even be possible to plan a "zero-waste" outing by carrying out everything when you depart.

Cooking Options. Will your outing involve cooking or open fires? There is a diverse array of outdoor cooking options. Portable stoves offer the easiest and least impactful cooking, and models range from lightweight backpacking stoves to larger dual-burner liquid or propane gas stoves. Next, consider cooking over charcoal, but make sure open flames are allowed. If you're using charcoal, burn it only within provided or allowed portable grills, and bring a container for carrying the cold and fully extinguished ashes to a disposal receptacle or back home.

Many significant and avoidable resource impacts are related to campfires, so choosing to build one involves additional responsibilities and

Food packaging can create unnecessary and avoidable waste when brought into the outdoors. Remove excess packaging before heading out to lighten your load and minimize the trash you must pack out. BEN LAWHON

skills to minimize impacts. Always check with landowners to see if and where campfires are permitted. Park and forest managers have documented numerous instances of highly invasive and destructive non-native insects being transported by visitors in their firewood brought from home; this practice is no longer recommended and is prohibited by an increasing number of states and protected areas. Insects, including larval grubs or eggs, along with fungal spores transported in wood, can infect local plants, causing devastating effects over time. If permitted, bringing scraps of preservative-free lumber from a home or commercial woodworking shop may be an option, but bringing artificial fire logs or purchasing wood at or near your campground are the best options.

Consider bringing gear like a metal fire pan to protect vegetation and soils by elevating your fire. Portable grills with short legs, metal oil pans or trashcan lids, or small satellite dishes elevated on large rocks make great fire pans. A variety of portable propane campfires and candle lanterns are also available, providing additional low-impact campfire options.

Finally, consider leaving some gear at home. Specifically, axes, hatchets, and saws can be useful in conservation projects but are no longer recommended and generally not necessary for camping. See more about this topic under the "Minimize Campfire Impacts" principle (page 53).

Food Storage Options. Whether you're picnicking or camping, bring adequate storage containers to protect all food, "smellables" (lotions, soaps, and odorous items), and trash from wildlife. Check with local land managers about which animals pose problems and the food storage practices they recommend, and then bring whatever gear is necessary to ensure safe storage. Large metal and plastic containers with securely clamped or screw-on lids are often acceptable in areas without bears. Vehicles are generally safe too. In bear country, some bears have learned to pry open back door windows and trunk lids to obtain food, so food storage inside vehicles is strictly prohibited in some areas. Inquire with managers about recommended storage options and practices, such as hanging bear bags or using metal storage lockers or other approved bearproof containers.

Toilet Options. Portable human waste facilities constitute a final "Leave No Trace Essentials" discussion topic. Consider bringing a portable toilet when camping in areas that lack them, particularly if vehicles, boats, or pack stock can carry them. Conduct an Internet search to learn about and evaluate portable toilet options; many are compact and lightweight, and some even have privacy screens. Backcountry visitors are increasingly encouraged, and in some areas required, to carry out their human waste. Search the Internet to learn about commercial pack-out toilet kits, which can be disposed of in a trashcan on your return. If you will be using the traditional cat-hole waste disposal method be sure to include a durable digging trowel. Finally, all feminine hygiene products must be disposed in a trashcan, never in toilets, cat-holes, or campfires.

Travel and Camp on Durable Surfaces

Research reveals that vehicle and trampling impacts to plants and soils occur quickly but these surfaces recover slowly. Minimize impact in popular areas by concentrating your activity on the most durable surfaces available, and in pristine areas by dispersing your activity so visible impacts never form.

Low-impact Driving Practices. Whether traveling to or from your recreation destination, or driving a vehicle, ATV, or motorcycle as part of your outdoor experience, you can avoid or minimize resource impacts by following a few simple low-impact driving practices. Most importantly, drive responsibly and stay on designated roads that are open to public use, or secure permission from private property owners. If driving off-road is acceptable and necessary, strive to do so only when soils are dry. Minimize your traffic and stick to the most durable surfaces available. Check with local land managers to determine the best driving routes and designated safe parking locations. Avoid driving on unsurfaced roads when conditions are muddy. Use only vehicles that can safely negotiate the roadbed without having to go around mud holes or other obstacles, as this substantially increases road width and impact. Yield to any horseback riders, hikers, and mountain bikers you encounter. Carry out all trash and check and wash your vehicle before and after trips to prevent the spread of non-native species. A thorough washing that removes all mud from the vehicles body and undercarriage is necessary to clean off non-native seeds. Additional low-impact vehicle use practices are available at the Tread Lightly website: www.treadlightly.org

Hardened trails are found in many areas and should be used whenever available. Sticking to these trails protects trailside plants and minimizes erosion. BEN LAWHON

Durable Surfaces

Durable and Nondurable Surfaces. Durable surfaces include pavement, rock, gravel, snow or ice, and barren soils on well-established trails and recreation sites. Concentrating your travel and activity on non-vegetated durable surfaces spares vegetation from being trampled and minimizes the signs of your visit. If durable surfaces are unavailable, use nonvegetated areas of organic litter (leaves, pine needles) or dry grassy meadows. Studies show that grasses are the most durable type of ground vegetation, particularly those growing in open sun on dry to moist (not wet) soils. Dry grassy fields are generally the best sites for large-group camping or picnic events.

Learn to recognize and avoid nondurable surfaces, including tall broadleafed herbs/forbs, ferns, wet soils, steep slopes, and biologic soil crust, also known as cryptobiotic soils. Most broad-leaved plants that grow in shade have stiff or weak stems that break easily, even under light traffic. In arid regions, cryptobiotic soils have a living "crust" of algae, cyanobacteria, fungi, lichens, and mosses. These crusts prevent soil erosion, retain soil moisture, and fix atmospheric nitrogen, but they are extremely fragile and easily damaged by traffic.

Actively seek out and use the most durable and resistant surface that's available to you for driving, riding, hiking, lunch or rest sites, and campsites. Explain what durable and nondurable surfaces are to your group and help them avoid areas of sensitive vegetation and soils.

Concentrate Activities on Established Trails and Recreation Sites. Research demonstrates that initial and low levels of trampling quickly remove most groundcover plants and organic litter, with substantial impact occurring in the first year of use. In contrast, recovery rates are very low, so the restoration of impacted trails and recreation sites to natural conditions can require ten to thirty years! An important implication of these findings is that *visitors should concentrate activity on formal or well-established trails and recreation sites and avoid expanding them or creating new ones.* Your group's impacts are likely to be substantially greater if you travel off-trail into pristine areas. Visiting these areas requires greater knowledge and experience of low-impact practices and considerable care to avoid the creation of lasting impact. For these reasons, only groups skilled in Leave No Trace dispersed-use practices should venture off the beaten path.

Be prepared to hike through snow, water, or mud. Going around such areas causes erosion, damage to trailside vegetation, and trail widening. DAVE WINTER

Concentrate Use in Popular Areas

In popular frontcountry or backcountry areas, concentrate your activities on marked formal or well-established trails and developed sites, including picnic areas, recreation and vista sites, and campsites. Staying on formal trails and well-established sites focuses your traffic on hardened or bare surfaces that resist further trampling impacts.

Preserve Trails. Seek out and use only marked or blazed trails in heavily used areas. Formal trails are usually sustainably designed, safer and easier to use, facilitate faster travel, and marked on maps so you are less likely to become lost. Studies show that most unmarked "informal" trails were created by visitors, and frequently degrade quickly and can impact sensitive or rare plant communities. Informal trail networks may also fragment wildlife habitats and hasten the dispersal of non-native plants. While some recreational pursuits require their use, such as accessing a fishing spot or climbing a crag, you can help preserve natural areas by minimizing the creation and use of these unofficial, unmarked, and sometimes illegal trails. If your activity requires travel away from formal trails in popular areas, it's best to find and travel on a well-used informal trail, unless you can stay on more durable rock or gravel surfaces. In particular, avoid using faint trails or areas where impacts are just beginning to show to promote their recovery.

Recognize that trails widen or form parallel paths when people walk on the edges, detour around obstacles, or walk side by side. Keep trails narrow and prevent these impacts by wearing appropriate footwear so you can walk single file in the center of trails—even where it's rocky or somewhat muddy (walk closely around the edges of deep mud holes if you must). If you are leaving deep prints (hoof, tire, or boot), the trail is too wet to use—find a drier alternative trail. Stay on the trail or a durable surface when passing others, or if others are passing you. Never shortcut a trail, especially on switchbacks, as steep shortcuts quickly erode into gullies, requiring costly restoration. Promote the recovery of closed trails and areas by avoiding them altogether.

Select Designated or Well-Established Campsites. When picnicking or camping in heavily used areas, choose only designated or legal well-established sites. Check with the land managers or owners for advice on selecting a site and on applicable camping regulations, permits, or low-impact practices. Some land managers require camping permits and use of designated sites; others simply promote the use of well-established campsites. For all activities, choose a spot you can use without enlarging it. If you have too many people or tents, divide into smaller groups and use additional sites. Confine your activities to the most durable and previously disturbed surfaces to avoid expanding a site's size. Preserve native vegetation by not stepping on plants and avoiding traffic in adjacent off-site areas. Most importantly, note that *recreation sites enlarged from just one group's use rarely return to their original size, as subsequent groups often continue using the newly expanded areas.*

Avoid creating new recreation sites or campsites and avoid using lightly impacted sites to promote their recovery. Recreation site and campsite proliferation are significant problems in many areas. Ask managers to identify likely possible locations that meet the needs of your group. Check for guidance on group sizes, number or placement of tents, food storage, campfires, and firewood sources. On campsites, place all tents, gear, and your cooking area near the center of your site. Consider using larger-capacity tents for youth groups to minimize your camping "footprint" and place them close together. Confining your activities to a core barren area keeps your site small, protects surrounding vegetation, and prevents development of disturbed "satellite" sites in offsite areas. However, in bear country it's advisable to separate the sleeping and cooking/food storage areas. Land managers generally provide special guidance on camping practices in bear country—inquire before visiting.

Good Campsites Are Found, Not Made. Spend time finding your perfect campsite; avoid remodeling or altering a site. For example, bring a lightweight chair instead of moving logs and rocks to sit on. Modern tents and sleeping pads allow greater flexibility and comfort in selecting a durable, dry, and comfortable tent site. Hammocks provide an even lower impact option, but when possible pitch them over a spot with little or no vegetation and use wide "tree-saver" straps instead of ropes, which can cut into tree bark. Trenching or removing vegetation when pitching tents and tarps is never appropriate. Portable stoves and even tables allow you to prepare meals anywhere without a campfire.

Protect trees and shrubs around your campsite from damage. Take care not to break off branches when securing tent, tarp, or clotheslines, and when suspending hammocks or food. Don't use wire or nails. If necessary, place a rolled-up stuff sack, an old piece of carpet, or other

Developed car camping sites offer amenities such as fire rings, picnic tables, hardened tent pads, and nearby toilets and trash receptacles, which make minimizing your impact easier. BEN LAWHON

padding under ropes to protect bark. Likewise, place lanterns where they will not singe bark. Even breaking off a tree branch for firewood creates an ugly scar and can expose the tree to insects and disease (see "Minimize Campfire Impacts," page 53, for information on collecting firewood). When camping with stock, use provided hitch rails, well-rigged high lines, portable fencing, cross-ties, or hobbles to restrain your animals without tying them directly to trees. Ask about the best stock confinement options for the area you plan to visit. Come prepared to confine your animals in a minimum-impact way.

Leave your campsite clean and natural looking—as *you* would like to find it. Remember that you are a host to those who use the site after your visit and they will notice your hospitality, or lack of it! Litter, graffiti, tree damage, exposed human and pet waste, spilled food, and unsightly fire rings are all *avoidable* impacts. By taking the time to pick up after yourself and others, you and the environment both benefit.

Large Group Activities. If you have a larger group, stick to popular areas and ask land mangers about the availability of group-use picnic or camping sites (which often require advance reservations). If such facilities are not available, secure approval to hold large group picnics or camping events in dry grassy fields. Be sure to have contingency plans for moving gear to and from the activity areas in the event of heavy or sustained rain or snow; otherwise vehicles can become stuck or create severe rutting damage. Monitor vegetation impacts and shift activities if you see the loss of vegetation cover beginning to occur.

Disperse Use in Pristine Areas

Does your recreational activity truly require off-trail travel or visiting pristine areas? If not, then stick to formal marked trails and recreation sites, whether in the frontcountry or backcountry. Recognize that the resource impacts of your visit on formal, designated trails and sites are often quite low. When you venture away from these impact-resistant trails and sites, the potential for harming natural resources is substantially higher. Accept the personal responsibility to Leave No Trace of your visit if you choose to venture off-trail.

When traveling off-trail, learn to "meadow-walk" by dispersing your traffic to avoid leaving a trace of your passage and creating new trails. JEFFREY MARION

Off-trail Hiking Practices. As previously noted, you may encounter informal (visitor-created) trails and sites, often only distinguishable from their formal counterparts by their lack of blazings, markings, or signs. Consult with land managers for specific guidance, but understand that off-trail traffic frequently leads to the proliferation of these informal networks of trails and sites. Furthermore, studies show that visitor-created trails and sites are more susceptible to resource impacts because they lack professional design, construction, and maintenance.

If your activity requires travel into pristine areas, or far away from formal trails and recreation sites, disperse your footsteps and activities to avoid repeat traffic and visible impact. If each person takes a slightly different route, a distinct trail won't form because no single plant receives multiple footfalls. Your objective in these areas is to avoid concentrated hiking or activity that leaves visible impact on plants and soils. Avoid using informal trails or recreation sites, particularly those that are not well used, to promote their recovery. Even a few passes by hikers or a single night of camping can substantially delay recovery to natural conditions. Because low levels of repeat traffic can create new trails and recreation sites, dispersal is generally an effective policy only in areas that receive low use.

Avoid Leaving Visible Impact. The degree of dispersal needed depends on the surfaces your group encounters. Rock surfaces that lack plant or lichen cover can tolerate concentrated traffic, as can barren gravel shorelines, dry washes, and snow or ice. Walking single file is acceptable only when doing so leaves no obvious disturbance to vegetation, organic litter, or soils. When traveling or camping in forests, find and use areas with the densest canopies that support little or no vegetation groundcover. When in doubt, periodically examine the effects of your group's activities and minimize impact by increasing dispersal or use of durable surfaces.

On nondurable surfaces, even low or inconsistent traffic along the same routes quickly leads to the development of informal, visitor-created trails. Cross-country hikers quickly discover that topography and vegetation acts to concentrate their traffic to routes with the fewest obstacles. Resist this tendency and keep your group broadly dispersed, with single-file traffic only on the most durable rock, gravel, or snow surfaces. Recognize that dispersed travel requires constant vigilance and is

Staying on durable surfaces, especially in high-use areas or in and around attractions, such as waterfalls, helps minimize impacts from trampling. BEN LAWHON

considerably slower and more difficult than hiking along a trail. Plan your schedule accordingly. Failure to disperse your group's traffic will accelerate the formation of informal trails that can quickly attract further use and impact.

Dispersed Camping. Dispersed or "pristine site" camping is generally not permitted or is discouraged in frontcountry areas as the potential for repeated use is simply too great. In less visited backcountry areas, camping impacts can be minimized by selecting the most durable and resistant spot available and by staying only one night at a particular site. Avoid *any* locations that show pre-existing camping disturbance to promote their recovery. When possible, also avoid areas that are highly visible to other visitors, vegetated shorelines, and areas with signs of wildlife. Moving a few sticks or rocks to erect a tent is fine, just return them before you depart. In forested areas hammocks make it even easier to Leave No Trace of your overnight stay.

Locate your cooking area on the most durable site available, like a large rock slab, gravel, or barren area. *Unless durable surfaces are available, avoid creating trails by limiting your trips and varying your route to water, sleeping, and cooking areas.* Monitor the effects of your activities, concentrating use on the most durable surfaces or dispersing your activities— whatever is necessary to avoid creating lasting impacts.

Before departing, naturalize and disguise the site—your objective is for no one to see or use the site again. Add leaf litter or pine needles to any scuffed-up areas. Fluff up flattened vegetation and organic material and replace any rocks or sticks you may have moved. If possible, place a log or branches across your tenting and cooking areas to deter their future use. Almost any forested setting can accommodate a single night of use each year without showing permanent effects; unvegetated or grassy areas can handle several nights. If you need to stay in one area longer, plan on moving your campsite when lasting vegetation or soil impacts begin to show.

Protect Water Resources. In most areas, sand and gravel bars along rivers or the ocean are durable surfaces that are generally suitable for dispersed camping. Avoid lakeshores and the banks of streams as such areas are often popular with hikers, anglers, or boaters, and their use is likely to attract repeated camping. Finding a secluded spot away from water with durable or nonvegetated surfaces is best, or a hidden grassy spot.

When traveling to get water take different routes and avoid steeper slopes that could erode soil into waterways. Where possible, also avoid camping near water in arid regions—these areas are ecologically important because they support diverse plant and animal populations that need water to survive in harsh dry environments. Additionally, plants and animals in arid environments are usually more sensitive to recreation disturbance.

Dispose of Waste Properly

Protect the areas you visit by accepting the responsibility to properly dispose of all wastes. Practice "Pack-it-in, pack-it-out!" Collect and carry out all trash and leftover food from your group and others. Make your outing a "trash-free" or "zero-waste" experience whenever possible.

Trash and Food

Accept responsibility to keep the areas you visit litter free and to prevent wildlife from obtaining your food or trash, including food wastes such as orange peels, eggshells, and coffee grounds. Carry plastic bags to collect trash and leftover food, and consider performing some community service by picking up and carrying out trash left by others. Always use wildlife-proof trash receptacles when available, or carry your trash home for proper disposal. If recycling containers are not available, bring items home to recycle and reduce the amount of waste that land managers must collect and dispose. If you have additional food, bring it home or give it directly to another visitor. Never leave food for other visitors hoping it will be consumed—this is worse than leaving trash, as wildlife are attracted to and will often eat unattended food.

Never Feed Wildlife. Wildlife should never be fed or permitted to obtain any human or pet food, or get into your trash, food waste, or other odorous toiletries. Be thorough in cleaning your site of all food. Even a few pieces of dropped granola or spilled noodles are sufficient to attract wild animals, including bears, which quickly lose their fear of humans and develop nuisance behaviors that may threaten your safety. Wildlife that obtain human food often develop strong attraction behaviors to trails, picnic areas, campsites, and visitors, turning wild animals into aggressive and potentially dangerous panhandlers. These food-conditioned animals pose a risk to humans and can damage packs and gear in search of food. Even the smells of flavored drinks can attract wildlife so consume drinks completely and remember that even the container can smell. Store all trash, food, spilled food, and odorous items (smellables) properly at all times to prevent access by wildlife. More information on this topic is included under the "Respect Wildlife" principle (page 63).

Carefully plan meal portions to avoid leftovers that will need to be disposed of in wildlife-proof trash receptacles or safely stored and taken home for proper disposal. Wildlife have a keen sense of smell and are attracted to all food smells—you can never completely burn food and oils or mask their smells, and buried food is easily located and dug up. Therefore, burning or burying food is never acceptable. Land managers report that wildlife seen visiting picnic areas and campsites generally head straight to campfire rings and often find something there to eat. Come prepared to pack out all trash and kitchen waste, particularly bacon grease, cooking oils, or other odorous byproducts of your cooking. A Forest Service study found that burning trash in campfires releases noxious fumes and produces ash with increased levels of a variety of harmful materials, including some that pose a threat to human health. Burning any trash or food is never wise.

Pack-It-In, Pack-It-Out. Before leaving any site where you've spent time, form a habit of carefully checking each area for belongings, trash, or food. Look for and retrieve any gear, like a bandana hanging in a tree, and "micro-garbage," such as dropped or spilled pieces of food and trash. Trash and litter are unsightly and can be deadly for animals. Even small items like cigarette butts are important to pick up and dispose in a trashcan. Cigarette butts in water release toxic chemicals that kill fish, and on the ground they take a decade to decompose. Wildlife frequently consume food wrappers, and fishing lines, hooks, and plastic products have ensnared or injured animals ranging from dogs to herons.

A final sweep is an easy and educational way to keep from "leaving a trace." Consider teaching outdoor ethics and stewardship to youth by inviting them to make a game or contest out of scavenging for "human

Pack-it-in, pack-it-out. Any food items, trash, and even biodegradable items need to be packed out. Burning trash is never a good idea as it releases toxins, rarely burns to ash, and can attract wildlife to fire sites unnecessarily. LEAVE NO TRACE CENTER FOR OUTDOOR ETHICS

sign." Even organic litter like orange peels and peanut hulls attract wildlife and can require more than a year to decompose; plastic and aluminum foil can last far longer, sometimes for many decades. If you carry it into the woods, then bring it out of the woods; otherwise it's simply litter!

Pet Waste

What's worse than smelling or seeing dog poop? Stepping in it! Pet wastes are an increasing problem in suburban and urban areas and can pose significant health threats to your family and pets, your neighbors, and local wildlife and water resources. As an example, think of cats. Cats can pose health threats to children when they bury their wastes in sandboxes, and they can transmit some diseases and parasites to wildlife. Consider the potential impacts of all pet wastes and accept the responsibility to remove them. Studies documenting the impacts of pet waste are increasingly leading to ordinances requiring pet owners to collect and properly dispose of pet wastes, or else face steep fines.

Bring plastic bags when you walk your dog—you can buy pet waste bags that clip to your leash or reuse newspaper, grocery store, or sandwich

ATTENTION ALL PETS!

Your waste can foul yards and play areas for children and threaten human health and water quality. According to the U.S. Centers for Disease Control (CDC), one day's dog waste can contain several billion fecal coliform bacteria, along with *Giardia* and the eggs of roundworms, hookworms, and tapeworms. Some bacteria and parasites can remain in the soil for years and still infect both humans and dogs. Children are particularly at risk from parasitic infected dog feces because they play barefoot—some larval worms can directly penetrate the skin. Studies have attributed pet wastes to instances of water pollution sufficient to exceed water quality standards, close beaches, and harm aquatic life. For example, a U.S. Geological Survey study in the Kansas City watershed found that pet waste is the source of approximately 25 percent of bacteria in local waterways.

bags. Put your hand inside the bag, pick up the pet waste, and pull the bag inside out, then seal in the waste and place it in a trashcan. Commercially available "pooper-scoopers" are also available. On overnight trips with your dog, another alternative is to deposit pet wastes in cat-holes following the guidance provided on pages 35–36. Always wash your hands after collecting pet waste. Keep your pet worm free and healthy through regular testing and deworming as needed.

Human Waste

When restrooms are present, use them, but be prepared if they are closed temporarily or seasonally. A wide variety of restroom facilities exist, ranging from primitive pit toilets with no privacy walls to composting toilets, vault toilets that are pumped out, and traditional flush toilets that send the wastes to drainage fields or sewage processing plants. Always look for, read, and follow any special guidance for their use. Regardless of the facility you find, there is one critical low-impact practice that's a constant: *Never put trash, leftover food, disposable wipes, diapers, or feminine hygiene products into toilets—all these items should be disposed of in a trashcan or carried home for proper disposal.* Toilets are *only* designed to handle human waste and toilet paper; all products other than toilet paper substantially interfere with the processing of the waste (flush and vault toilets) or the decomposition process (pit and composting toilets). Signs on some composting toilets may direct you to throw in a few handfuls of organic mulch or leaf litter after each use to aid the decomposition process. Park and forest managers provide these facilities for your convenience—assist them by using toilets properly.

Practice good sanitation when using toilets; wash your hands thoroughly with soap and water to avoid transmitting bacteria or viruses to others. If hand washing is not possible, use an antibacterial gel. Keep the toilet area clean and free of trash—leave it as *you* would like to find it!

When toilets are unavailable, answering nature's call involves a little pre-planning and additional work to avoid some significant impacts. Proper disposal of human waste is important to maximize the rate of decomposition, avoid the spread of diseases such as *Giardia*, salmonella, and dysentery, minimize pollution of water sources, and reduce the negative implications of someone else finding it.

Portable Toilets. In areas that lack public restrooms, consider bringing a portable toilet. A variety of inexpensive portable toilets are available, ranging from lightweight and compact models to those with battery-operated flush systems. Some compact versions use lightweight folding legs, snap-on seats, and plastic sealable, leak-proof bags to hold wastes. Other models use a standard 5-gallon bucket lined with a plastic bag and snap-on seat. Heavier designs include toilet bowls, water tanks with flush systems, and a waste-holding tank underneath. Tentlike privacy shelters can be used with many portable toilets. Wastes can be disposed by emptying the contents at a waste-disposal facility or into a flush toilet, or bagged and deposited into approved trash facilities. For the latter option, chemical and enzyme products are available that gel liquids, speed the breakdown of solid waste, and deodorize. These products *must be used*, and in accordance with the manufacturer's directions, for this option to be effective and legal.

Cat-holes. When toilets are unavailable, the recommended "best practice" for solid human or pet waste disposal below the tree line is to deposit it in "cat-holes." Dig these 6 to 8 inches deep and 4 to 6 inches in diameter at least 200 feet (80 steps) from water, trails, and campsites. Good cat-hole sites keep waste well away from all areas of visitor use and water sources, including lakes, streams, springs, and low areas such as dry ravines that fill with water during rainstorms. Avoid damage to plants and speed decomposition by selecting a less vegetated site with thick organic soils. Whenever possible, reduce high concentrations of cat-holes near campsites by selecting a remote location during the day's travel.

Bring a trowel to dig the hole, or use a stout stick. Waste burial under flat rocks hinders decomposition. Burying waste in a 6- to 8-inch-deep hole helps ensure that it will not be carried to a water source during storms, seen by other visitors, or accessed by flies that could spread diseases. When possible use unbleached, non-scented toilet paper and check on local guidance for properly disposing of used toilet paper. If you bury it, use a stick to push it deep in the hole to deter animals from digging it up. Studies show that buried toilet paper decomposes in 1 to 3 years except in areas with particularly cold, wet, or dry soils (e.g., alpine areas, wetlands, deserts). Always carry out disposable wipes, diapers, or feminine hygiene products as these items attract wildlife and decompose very slowly. Alternatively, consider packing your used toilet paper out in doubled plastic bags. Burning toilet paper at a cat-hole is not recommended as it can lead to wildfires.

When finished, use your trowel or a stick to completely cover the toilet paper and waste with several inches of dark organic soil (when available). Mixing the waste with organic soil, which is biologically active with decomposer organisms, greatly accelerates decomposition. Disguise the hole and cover it with leaf litter and a branch to deter traffic around it.

Soil microbes will decompose human waste but studies reveal that pathogens can remain viable for up to two years in cat-holes, hence the importance of cat-hole placement away from water and deep burial. Do not leave human waste or toilet paper on the surface or under surface rocks—if the cat-hole method is ill suited to your group, camp where an outhouse or restrooms are available, or bring a portable toilet.

Lastly, it is always a good idea to check local regulations for disposing of human or pet waste as recommended practices often vary from one location to the next.

Latrines. If you're traveling with young children or group camping for many nights in the same site, it might be best to dig a latrine, unless you can use a portable toilet. Site the latrine as you would a cat-hole, 200 feet

A good cat-hole site is at least 200 feet away from water sources, campsites, and trails. Use a trowel to dig a 6- to 8-inch hole, making sure to keep the trowel clean. Once the waste is in the hole, cover with dirt and disguise the area. BEN LAWHON (TOP) AND LEAVE NO TRACE CENTER FOR OUTDOOR ETHICS (BOTTOM)

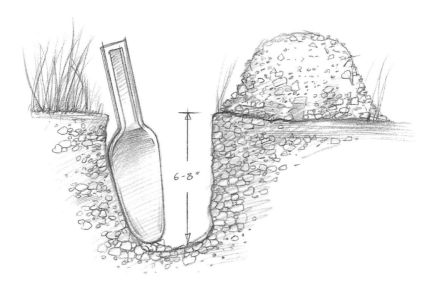

(80 steps) from water, campsites, and trails, and make sure that the route to the latrine is over durable surfaces. Dig a trench 6 to 8 inches deep and long enough to accommodate the needs of your party. When available, add organic soil and surface litter after each use. Bury the toilet paper deeply or pack it out. Naturalize the site before leaving and add brush to deter traffic.

Carryout Options. Strive to make your outdoor adventure a "zero-waste" trip by carrying out all wastes, including human waste. Land managers are increasingly recommending or requiring visitors to carry out their human waste, particularly in environments where it is extremely difficult to operate toilets or allow cat-holes, such as high elevations, deep river canyons, deserts, or arctic areas with permafrost. Cliff environments, caves, and slickrock areas represent additional settings where carryout recommendations and regulations are common. In all these special environments, human wastes have a higher probability of polluting water or won't decay because of a lack of appropriate soils or moisture, or extreme cold or heat. Carrying out human wastes is the recommended "best practice" in all these special settings.

Carryout options range from portable toilets to a wide variety of commercial or homemade bag systems and "poop tubes." Always check with local land managers and follow their recommendations on the most appropriate carryout system and disposal practice. Boating and pack animal trips will generally allow the use of reusable/washable portable toilets, while hikers and backpackers can use lightweight systems composed of doubled plastic biodegradable bags, with gels and enzymes (conduct a web search on "human waste disposal bag"). Climbers and cavers generally opt for more rigid poop tubes, while mountaineers use bags or larger reusable plastic containers. The wastes can be placed in a waste disposal facility, a flush toilet (no plastic bags), or for bag systems, in an approved trash receptacle. If a bag system is used, the chemical and enzyme products *must be used* in accordance with the manufacturer's directions for this option to be effective and legal. Always check with local land managers to find out an appropriate disposal method for the area you plan to visit.

Urine. Although typically not a health concern, concentrated urine smells, attracts animals, and has the potential to harm plants and water resources. Studies indicate that when widely dispersed, urine poses few impacts of concern. However, visitors often select the same places to urinate, for example behind a large rock or shrub or a few steps from a tentsite or trail shelter. This results in high concentrations of urine. Noxious smells, concentrated urea, and excess nutrients in these locations do pose problems. For example, urea salts and ammonia byproducts could harm aquatic life in small or slow-moving water bodies, alter soil chemistry, and damage plant leaves. The noxious smells of concentrated urine are particularly unpleasant to other visitors. Wildlife are attracted to the salts in urine, and in their effort to obtain them may defoliate plants and disturb soils. Avoid these impacts by using restroom facilities when available, noting that some types of composting toilets can't accommodate large amounts of urine (look for guidance). When away from facilities, urinate at least 100 feet (40 steps) away from water, trails, campsites, and recreation sites. Avoid commonly used spots and choose a nonvegetated surface whenever possible, such as organic litter, sand, and gravel, or grass in vegetated areas.

Hygiene for Women. In areas without toilets or suitable privacy, consider using a poncho and an out-of-the-way spot for bathroom-related activities. Always be prepared to deal with your period by bringing unscented hygiene products with supplies to pack them out. Tampons and menstrual pads are generally made of synthetic fibers or have plastic wraps that resist decomposition, as do disinfecting wipes. Studies show these items can survive for many years when buried so pack them out for disposal. A simple disposal method is to wrap the items in some toilet paper and a square of aluminum foil and double bag in Ziploc bags. If odors are a problem, place crushed aspirin or tea bags inside. Most female backpackers find tampons to be the smallest and least bulky to pack out. Menstrual cups are another option but try them at home before using them on an outdoor trip. While effective, these cups can be messy and require daily cleaning. Pack out the menstrual fluid using one of the commercially available human waste disposal bags if feasible, or bury it using the cat-hole method. In bear country, these items must be safely stored with your food, trash, and other smellables—burning these items to ash is very difficult and not a recommended option. Research and evaluations of encounters between bears and humans have found no compelling evidence that black and grizzly bears are attracted by menstrual blood, though polar bears appear to be an exception. Finally, for daily hygiene needs, consider using a bandana or small washcloth instead of cleansing wipes (which must be packed out). Clean reusable cloths away from water sources.

Lotions, Sprays, and Powders. We put many products on our skin, including sunscreen, deodorants and antiperspirants, lotions, bug spray, scented soap, foot powder, perfume, make-up, and lip balm. Take precautions to avoid spilling these products and to rinse them off prior to swimming. All of these products should be considered smellables and stored out of reach of all animals when not traveling or when in use. While there is no research-based guidance on their use in bear country, some precautionary guidance is possible:

+ Bring only the products you really need.
+ Use unscented versions but recognize that even these could attract bears.
+ Use them only when necessary, preferably in the morning rather than later in the day.
+ Consider a soap and water wash-up at night before bed and sleeping in a "clean" set of clothing.

Special Environments. Always check with local land managers for specific guidance when recreating in special environments.

Snow, Arctic, and Alpine Environments: Snow and frozen soils generally prevent cat-hole use in cold weather. Many alpine environments have little soil, and cold temperatures prevent decomposition of the wastes. Poop tubes, bag systems, or other pack-out options are best for disposal. When it's cold enough for the waste to freeze, packing it out is fairly easy. When winter camping in more temperate areas, you may be able to locate a patch of exposed ground, usually under a tree, where a trowel can penetrate the snow and duff.

Waterways: Carrying a portable toilet is standard practice on many waterways and may be required by land managers. Site the toilet on a durable spot where no new trails will be created to reach it. Where land is limited, like in deep river canyons, diluting urine by peeing into the waters of a high-volume river is also often an acceptable practice. Check local regulations.

Desert Lands: Consider carrying out your waste in deserts, as conditions are generally too dry for wastes to decompose. Otherwise, locate cat-holes following standard guidance, avoiding dry washes and favoring rarely visited sites with maximum sun exposure where the sun's heat can penetrate desert soils to desiccate and kill pathogens.

Coastal Areas: If you are boating, carry a portable toilet or a bag system to carry out human waste and urinate in the water if permitted. In remote coastal areas digging a cat-hole more than 200 feet (80 steps) from shore is an acceptable alternative.

Wastewater

Washing your dishes, body, hair, or clothing, or even cooking or brushing your teeth, produces wastes that must be disposed of properly. The chief concerns are pollution of water resources and attraction of wildlife. In developed areas, check with local managers and follow their guidance. For example, restroom sinks in campgrounds are generally reserved for washing hands, brushing teeth, and shaving. Washing dishes at restroom sinks may be discouraged or prohibited, though some facilities have utility sinks or water faucets with sumps for these activities. Never pour unstrained graywater (cooking water or dishwater), cooking oils, or coffee grounds into sinks or on the ground. Toilets that flush are good venues for disposing of strained dishwater. Leave any public facilities clean following your use and be sure to remove any food scraps from sumps or drain sieves and put them in the trash. Be familiar with local regulations: while 100 feet (40 steps) is a guideline for the proper distance for dispersing wastewater away from campsites and trails, some areas require a greater distance (200 feet), the common distance away from water sources and campsites for burying human waste.

Washing Dishes. Dishwashing begins before dinner ends by encouraging everyone to consume *all* of their food, down to the last scrap or grain of rice. If someone can't finish their meal, or that final scoop from the cook pot, every group generally has at least one "human garbage disposal" that can be coaxed into finishing it. Scrape off and carry out *all* remaining food from pots and plates. Most dishes can be cleaned with a little water, a few drops of soap, and a scouring pad (sponges can't remove burned food and they retain bacteria). Use unscented phosphate-free biodegradable soap, recognizing that even these soaps contain chemicals that are harmful to water sources. Most soaps require six months to several years to biodegrade, so use them sparingly, and never use them in or near natural water sources. Remove any grease or oil from dishes with some toilet paper or a paper towel, followed by hot water and a few drops of soap directly on the scouring pad.

If you sanitize dishes, do so by dipping them in boiling water for 30 seconds. You can dip them in the boiling water used to prepare your next meal. Alternately, sanitize items by submerging them in chemically treated cold water (unscented chlorine bleach, 1.5 teaspoons per gallon) for at least 1 full minute (*note:* water over 115°F stops bleach from sanitizing). Rinse dishes in clean water and air dry. Strain cooking water and

A four-bucket wash system is an easy way to clean dishes in the outdoors. River, horse-back, and car camping trips—and even picnics—are well suited to this type of dish-washing. Straining all remaining food particles from dishwater before disposal is imperative. BEN LAWHON

dishwater through a piece of fiberglass screen or mesh strainer to remove any food particles and pack them out. Prevent animals from obtaining any food waste, including small "micro-garbage," for reasons discussed under the "Respect Wildlife" principle (page 63).

Dispose of the *strained* cooking, dishwashing, and chemically treated sanitizing water in a sink, noncomposting (flush) toilet, or sump hole when possible. Do not use pit or composting toilets (outhouses) to deposit dishwater as the food odors can attract animals that will damage the outhouse, and excess water slows or halts the decomposition of wastes. In areas without washing facilities, carry strained liquids at least 100 feet (40 steps) away from any water resources or campsites to protect water quality and avoid attracting wildlife. A preferred disposal method is to filter these liquids through a screen and scatter them widely by fling-ing it in a broad dispersing arc, known as "broadcasting." Alternatively pour strained cooking or dishwashing water into the soil, preferably

Use a mesh or kitchen strainer to remove all food particles from dishwater before disposal. All particles should be placed in the trash and packed out. LEAVE NO TRACE CENTER FOR OUTDOOR ETHICS

under some thick organic litter to mask smells. Avoid killing soil microorganisms letting boiling water cool prior to disposal.

Personal Hygiene. Frequent hand washing with soap has been shown to be the most effective practice for reducing illnesses in outdoor settings. Wash your hands at least 100 feet (40 steps) away from water sources and use small amounts of unscented phosphate-free biodegradable soap, rinsing in the same spot. In particular, wash your hands prior to preparing or eating food and after any "bathroom" trips. Hand-sanitizing gels can be substituted but these may be less satisfactory when hands are particularly dirty. For shaving and washing hair or bodies, carry water away from campsites and at least 100 feet from water sources. Where fresh water is scarce, think twice before swimming in creeks or potholes. Lotion, sunscreen, insect repellent, and body oils can contaminate these vital water sources. Remove these chemicals from your skin by rinsing off at least 100 feet from water sources before swimming.

For brushing teeth away from sinks, try using a small amount of toothpaste and consider swallowing your rinse water. Otherwise walk at least 100 feet from campsites, spit in one spot and pour additional water until the spot is gone, or use a "broadcast" spit to disperse the rinse water over a wide area.

Fish and Game Entrails

Check with local managers for guidance when disposing of the remains of fish or game animals. The best option is to bring them out for proper disposal. Double bag fish entrails to prevent odor and spillage; store them out of the reach of animals. Leaving fish remains along shorelines encourages food attraction behaviors by wildlife, turning them into aggressive panhandlers. If entrails can't be carried out, bury them more than 200 feet (80 steps) away from trails, campsites, and water sources. Disposal of fish entrails in the water can perpetuate some fish diseases and campfires are rarely successful for burning them entirely to ash. Larger wildlife carcasses can generally be left on the ground surface for other animals to consume as long as they are far away from camps, trails, and water sources.

Leave What You Find

Observe, photograph, and learn about the rocks, plants, wildlife, and natural and cultural artifacts you see during your outdoor visits, but leave them "as found" for others to enjoy. Help preserve the special qualities of the areas you visit by "leaving what you find," and pass the gift of discovery on to those who follow.

Consider your last outdoor visit and what made it "special" to you. Could it have been the turtle or lizard you saw along the trail, an amazing display of native flowers, or a fascinating fossil, arrowhead, or archaeological ruin? Many of us learned about and grew to love nature and wildlife by taking care of pet amphibians or reptiles. However, numerous studies have documented the potential harm that we can do when we collect and take home native wildlife, pick trailside flowers, or collect artifacts and other natural objects to keep as mementos of our visits. "Leaving what you find" can be challenging but consider this: What if everyone took home a desired natural object? Would your outdoor adventures be as "special" if you failed to see such treasures?

Observe It, Photograph It, and Leave It

When we go on vacations, we frequently purchase a souvenir to keep and display as a reminder of our visit. Outdoor visitors are equally tempted to collect and take home interesting natural and cultural objects, but such acts are rarely sustainable if *everyone* does the same. Such collecting has the potential to do substantial harm, so resist the urge and teach

Petroglyph panels such as these are cultural treasures that should be respected. Refrain from touching or altering these ancient carvings. Photographs, sketches, or paintings are the best way to remember such sites. BEN LAWHON

others to do the same. Consider the adage, "Take only photographs and leave only footprints." Substitute a photograph or sketch to share or display your "find" and enable you to identify and learn more about it after your trip. Take home memories instead of souvenirs to ensure that those who follow have the same high-quality experience you enjoyed. Fill your memory card, not your backpack!

There are many reasons for leaving special objects behind. Consider the cumulative effect of millions of visitors to our public lands. If we each picked a few flowers or took a cactus, fossil, or pet home with us, the cumulative effect would be devastating. Instead, load your camera. Let photos, drawings, and memories comprise your souvenirs. People come to public lands to enjoy them in a natural and pristine state. Allow others a sense of discovery by leaving plants, artifacts, and other objects of interest as you find them. Bring children and introduce them to the wonders of nature but help them to understand the interconnectedness of plants, animals, and natural environments. Teach youth that picking

With more people spending time in the outdoors, it is important that we leave natural, cultural, and historic objects as they are found. Fill your memory card, not your pack.
BEN LAWHON

flowers prevents the development of seeds, which produce next year's plants and flowers. For example, a study in Great Smoky Mountains National Park found significantly fewer pink lady slipper orchids flowering along park trails than away from trails. Educate youth on stewardship and their personal responsibility to preserve these important resources by leaving them where they are found so that others may discover, experience, and enjoy them as they did.

Respect Wildlife by Leaving It Alone. Consider box turtles, which have traditionally been popular pets. Did you know that box turtles can live over one hundred years in the wild but rarely survive a year or two in captivity? Box turtle populations have declined markedly in recent decades, partly because people are collecting them in large numbers to keep or sell as pets. The same is true for many other reptiles and amphibians collected in the wild, including toads, frogs, snakes, and lizards, which also suffer shortened life spans as pets. Few youth know enough about their pet's habitat and dietary needs, which can be highly specific.

Exercise stewardship instead of ownership by ensuring that your activities do not diminish the ability of other species to survive.

Many states have passed laws making it illegal to collect wild animals, including amphibians and reptiles, without special permits. The ethical option for youth who want to raise such pets is to purchase *only* captive-bred animals from responsible retailers. Wildlife biologists also stress that only healthy native wildlife caught in the wild and kept as pets should be released, and only in the exact location where caught. Captive-bred animals lack the knowledge to forage for food or escape predators, or may carry harmful diseases that infect native animals. Although it may seem reasonable to release unwanted pets in natural areas, doing so can introduce harmful pathogens and parasites, disrupt the local ecology, and condemn the abandoned pet to a slow death. The release of non-native animals has led to substantial impacts to native flora and fauna in several regions of the United States. Prevent these impacts by selling or giving your unwanted pets to the place where you bought them or to a school, nature center, or zoo—never release them into the wild.

Leaving Your Mark. Respect nature and leave it as you found it—this is the true essence of Leave No Trace. Good campsites are found, not made. When you alter a site or move and rearrange logs, rocks, or other features you are altering natural habitats and creating unnatural scenes for visitors who follow you. Accept nature on its terms and ensure that those in your group don't litter, alter natural features, damage trees, create new campfire sites, or carve or write graffiti on rocks or park structures and signs. If you have time and can perform some community service, consider picking up trash or disassembling and dispersing constructed camp tables or elaborate chairs and rock "artwork" in backcountry settings. If in doubt, check with land managers for guidance.

Harvesting: If you plan to fish, hunt, or collect a large quantity of berries or other natural items always check with local land managers on regulations, permits, and guidance. Ask about harvest limits, the best method for disposing of animal remains, safety practices, and what types of collecting are not permitted.

Cairns. Stacks of rocks called cairns are used to mark trails and guide hikers in the mountains above the tree line, in open areas that lack trees, or in trail-less areas. Never create unauthorized new routes or cairns, dismantle existing cairns on formal routes, or add rocks to cairns. Limiting your traffic to formal routes in alpine and subalpine environments is critical to protecting sensitive plants; if trampled, they can require decades to recover because of short growing seasons. When you create new routes or cairns you greatly expand trampling impacts and misdirect visitors from official routes into more fragile or dangerous areas, particularly in the winter when trails are hidden by snow. Finally, the removal of rocks to build or add to cairns makes mountain soils more prone to erosion in an environment where new soil creation requires thousands of years.

Preserve the Past

You are likely to encounter historic, archaeological, or fossil sites during your visits to public lands. These sites are special places that tell the story of our past. Historic resources are those that are more than fifty years old, and include structures, equipment, and artifacts from old mining, logging, or homestead sites. Archaeological and historical structures and artifacts are reminders of our rich human history. When damaged or stolen, these irreplaceable resources are gone forever. Be aware that the Archaeological Resources Protection and National Historic Preservation Acts make it illegal to disturb archaeological or historic sites or remove any artifacts—including potsherds, arrowheads, mining tools, or antique bottles. Archaeological sites represent our only source of knowledge about prehistoric humans and the most valuable sites are those preserved intact since being abandoned. Similarly, removal of fossils or petrified wood can result in the loss of scientific information or diminish the quality of recreational experiences for other visitors.

Look But Don't Touch! These fragile heritage resources are not always readily visible so be especially careful when visiting areas where they occur. Observe or photograph heritage resources but do not disturb, touch, or take them. Consider the *permanent* cumulative effect if thousands of visitors took "just one" item. Preserve America's priceless heritage exactly as you find it. Treat heritage sites with respect, as Native Americans consider many sites sacred. Allow future visitors the same sense of discovery; even picking up or moving artifacts takes them out of context and diminishes their archaeological value. Be careful to avoid *any* ground disturbance by staying on trails, not climbing on ruins, and camping well away from heritage sites. Admire and photograph rock art

Natural objects like this moose antler are exciting to find outdoors. Resist the temptation to remove such items, as they are a natural part of the environment and should be left where found. BEN LAWHON

but do not touch or add to it—graffiti is vandalism that forever damages pictographs and petroglyphs.

If you see someone stealing artifacts or digging at heritage sites, observe and record (from a distance) their physical description, location, activities, and license plate number, and call 911 to report it *as soon as possible.* Many heritage sites are in remote areas that are difficult to monitor and enforce. You can help protect your heritage by reporting crimes or suspicious activity.

Avoid Spreading Non-native Plants and Animals

Non-native or exotic plants and animals are those that were not originally indigenous to a particular area—that is, they were transported and introduced to a new area, generally by humans. Non-native "invasive" species are those that out-compete and replace native species over large areas. The negative effects on ecological conditions and biodiversity can be significant, and highly invasive species cause substantial economic impacts. For example, ecological studies have discovered that introduced earthworms, including "bait" worms released by anglers, have altered the soil and nutrient conditions of entire forests, causing reduced forest

Check and clean shoes, clothing, and gear to avoid introducing non-native and invasive plant seeds into protected areas. JEFFREY MARION

organic litter and plant groundcover, increased erosion rates, and a reduction in the number and diversity of native insects. The estimated damage and control costs of invasive species in the United States alone amount to more than $138 billion annually.

You can help prevent the spread of non-native species where you live and on outings by following these actions:

+ Learn more about non-native species in your area, what they look like, and prevention and control measures. Many resources are available on the Internet. Search them out!

+ Look for and control non-native plants in your yard, including "invasive ornamentals" that commonly escape our yards to invade nearby woods and fields.

+ Contact local parks and forests to volunteer your assistance in efforts to remove non-native species.

+ Never release unwanted pets or leftover live fishing bait.

+ Carefully inspect and clean your boats, trailers, vehicles, outdoor gear, clothing, footwear, and pets or livestock to remove clinging vegetation, insects and egg cases, burrs, seeds, and mud prior to visiting another protected natural area.

+ Use weed-free feed for horses and pack-stock for three days prior to your protected area visit.

+ Never transport firewood—it may contain invasive insects or diseases that kill trees.

Minimize Campfire Impacts

Land managers are increasingly prohibiting campfires because of their many associated impacts. However, most of these are entirely avoidable. Do your part by adopting safe and low-impact campfire practices, or consider not having a campfire.

Public land managers frequently cite a long list of resource impacts attributable to campfires, including the following:

+ extensive off-site trampling of vegetation associated with firewood collection,
+ large areas near campsites barren of all wood,
+ axes, hatchets, and saws used to damage and fell trees and shrubs, including live trees and dead snags important to wildlife, and
+ large trashy fire pits overflowing with charcoal and ash, and partially burned food or cooking oils that attract wildlife, which can endanger campers.

For example, a research study of backcountry campsites in Great Smoky Mountains National Park found 2,377 damaged trees and 3,366 cut tree stumps. These unnecessary and avoidable impacts have prompted nearly half of National Park Service backcountry managers to prohibit campfires, and most also prohibit the cutting of standing dead trees. If visitors learn to avoid these impacts by adopting the low-impact campfire practices recommended under this principle, perhaps these campfire prohibitions might one day be lifted.

Fires can be destructive and often leave long-lasting scars on the landscape. Use existing fire rings whenever available, and keep your fires safe and manageable. LEAVE NO TRACE CENTER FOR OUTDOOR ETHICS

Choosing to Have a Campfire

Given the higher potential of campfires to cause lasting resource impacts, first ask yourself if you really need a campfire. The development of efficient, lightweight camp stoves for cooking has encouraged a shift away from the traditional campfire. Portable stoves are easy to use, fast, and clean burning; they operate reliably in almost any weather condition; and they avoid all campfire-related resource impacts. Most campers now use portable stoves for cooking food so campfires are more commonly built as a focus of social gatherings and sometimes for warmth or to dry wet clothing. Some advantages of using a candle lantern to light an evening gathering are that you will avoid breathing smoke all evening or getting holes in clothing or tents from flying embers.

However, for some visitors, having a campfire is an important and traditional element of a high-quality camping experience. Recognize that choosing to build a campfire involves additional responsibilities and skills to minimize the impact. Always check with land managers to see if and where campfires are permitted, and for campfire management guid-

For many, campfires are an integral part of any camping experience. Only build fires when and where they are allowed, when conditions are safe, and when you have the skills necessary to manage your fire. BEN LAWHON

ance. Consider the following issues in making your decision and choose not to have a campfire when circumstances are unfavorable.

- ✦ Are campfires legal and safe to build at this location and time? (Note that campfires are unsafe and may be prohibited during times of higher fire danger, or are inadvisable during dry or windy conditions.)
- ✦ Is there an existing campfire site? If not, do you have the knowledge to build and remove all traces of a campfire? Always refrain from building new campfire sites or moving existing ones.
- ✦ Is there an adequate supply of firewood or can you purchase firewood from a local source? High elevation, arctic, and desert environments do not generate sufficient firewood to support campfires.
- ✦ Will you be able to safely manage the campfire and completely extinguish it before departing?
- ✦ Do group members possess the skill to build a campfire that will Leave No Trace?

Campfire Types and Locations

The easiest and best option is to build a campfire in a legal pre-existing fire grate, ring, or rock fire pit. Consider that campfires commonly produce flying embers that can ruin tents or even set them on fire if too close. Except in emergencies, do not move or create a new fire site unless you remove all traces when you're done. There are many types of campfire options and low-impact practices vary accordingly.

Existing Fire Sites. The best place to build a campfire is within an existing fire ring; if there are multiple fire sites, choose the one away from the best tenting areas. Never use fire sites near rock outcrops, archaeological or historic sites, or trees and exposed roots. Don't enlarge or add rocks to fire rings.

Fire Pans/Portable Gas Fires. Metal fire pans elevated high enough to protect vegetation and soils provide another good low-impact campfire option. Commercial fire pans, barbecue grills, and metal oil drain pans or trashcan lids make effective fire pans. Elevate the pan on large rocks or line it with 4 to 5 inches of mineral soil so the heat will not scorch vegetation beneath. A variety of portable propane campfires are also available, providing additional low-impact campfire options. Locate your campfire in a resistant area that lacks vegetation and organic litter whenever possible to avoid the trampling impacts of your group.

Beach/Gravel Fires. Some areas permit campfires on nonvegetated sand or gravel beaches, preferably below the high tide or seasonal high water line. When done, fully extinguish the fire and widely scatter all ashes and charcoal to remove all traces of your campfire.

Mound Fires. This type of fire requires more substantial effort and a large source of mineral soil from an uprooted tree, or sand or gravel from a nonvegetated location. Fill a large stuff sack turned inside out and deposit the material on a ground cloth or fire blanket placed in a resistant area, preferably with little to no vegetation and organic litter. Use sufficient material to create a flat-topped mound roughly 2 feet in diameter and about 8 inches thick to insulate the ground (4 inches for small fires built with twigs). When done, completely extinguish the fire, scatter the ashes and charcoal, return the soil to its source, and thoroughly naturalize the site.

Pit Fires. When the options above are unavailable, a campfire can be built in a shallow excavated pit. Avoid or take special precautions in locations with vegetation, leaf litter, organic soils, or roots that might catch

Fire pans made of metal offer a good way to avoid scorching the ground. Elevate your pan on rocks and keep your fire small enough to be contained in the pan. Stoves are often easier to use for cooking since they work regardless of weather and leave no mess to clean up when finished. BEN LAWHON (TOP) AND LEAVE NO TRACE CENTER FOR OUTDOOR ETHICS (BOTTOM)

fire. Dig and set aside plugs of soil. If vegetation is present, be sure to extract intact root balls and keep them adequately watered. Thoroughly extinguish the fire, scatter all ashes and charcoal, return the excavated material, re-water any vegetation, and fully naturalize the site to deter future use.

Gathering Firewood

Many avoidable campfire-associated impacts are related to firewood collection. Campgrounds and backcountry campsites often develop a barren, "camped-out" appearance because all available dead wood within reach is missing, and because many trees and shrubs have been cut down or damaged by axes, hatchets, or saws. New infestations of invasive tree-killing insects and diseases often occur in camping areas because visitors have brought infected firewood from home. A few simple low-impact practices will allow you to prevent these impacts.

Gather Only Small Pieces of Dead and Downed Wood. Live wood does not burn and dead wood from live or dead trees provides vital habitat and food for native insects and animals, so leave them intact. Cutting or breaking branches off standing or fallen trees creates an aesthetically displeasing "human browse line" that detracts from an area's natural appearance. *The "best practice" for firewood collection is to collect only dead and downed wood you can easily break by hand in areas with a plentiful wood supply.* As a general rule of thumb, collect wood from the ground that is smaller in diameter than your wrist and sufficiently dry to easily snap by hand or underfoot. Larger-diameter wood provides important habitat for forest insects, a critical source of food for birds and wildlife, and homes for cavity-nesting birds and small mammals. If you can't find plentiful firewood then purchase firewood locally, consider appropriate alternative campfire fuels (see the next page), or forgo having a campfire.

Leave Woods Tools at Home. The felling and damage of trees and shrubs from axes, hatchets, and saws are perhaps the most significant ecological and aesthetic impacts related to campfires. Woods tools are also responsible for many serious camping injuries. These impacts and injuries are *entirely avoided* by not using woods tools when camping, *as recommended by most public land managers.* Use them only when doing conservation work, like trail maintenance. At campsites, such tools are invariably used to cut down trees, saplings, or shrubs, or to wound them, allowing subsequent rot and invasion by insects or diseases that weaken or kill them. By enabling the burning of large-diameter wood, these tools also contribute to unnecessarily large and unsightly campfires that produce substantial amounts of ash, charcoal, and partially burned wood that quickly fill fire rings. Leaving woods tools at home protects live trees and dead snags that are important to wildlife. It also lightens your load and enhances the safety of your group.

Don't Move Firewood. Collect or purchase wood where you burn it. Transporting firewood long distances for camping or woodstove/fireplace burning increases the risk of introducing invasive insects and diseases moved with the wood. Many public land managers now prohibit campers from transporting wood. Many point out that new infestations of nonnative tree-killing insects and diseases are often first found in their campgrounds. The specific insects and diseases of concern vary by region but some have already killed millions of trees over thousands of acres. You can help stop the spread of these invasive insects by buying wood at the campground or bringing alternative campfire fuels. Even wood that looks clean can have tiny insects or eggs in the loose bark, or microscopic fungal spores that will escape to start a new and deadly infestation.

Consider Alternative Campfire Fuels. In addition to charcoal, an increasing diversity of campfire logs made from recycled compressed sawdust and wood products are available for campfires. These products avoid the risk of transporting insects and diseases and have a number of advantages for campers. They produce very little smoke, emit no flying embers to damage clothing or tents or start wildfires, and burn more cleanly with fewer particulates, less carbon monoxide, and no petrochemicals or noxious fumes. They also have twice the density of cordwood, providing long burn times.

Managing Your Campfire

Regardless of the type of campfire you have, there are some simple practices that will help you have a safe and low-impact campfire.

Burn Only Wood. Carry out rather than burn any type of trash, cooking oils, and leftover food, which create unsightly fire rings and can produce noxious fumes or smells that attract wildlife like skunks and bears. Studies have found an array of unnatural chemicals and residues in campfire ashes, including dangerous heavy metals and poisons that pollute the environment. Wildlife biologists report that bears frequently visit campsite fire rings first and invariably find some interesting smell or item of food or trash to eat there. *You can prevent all these impacts by burning only wood.*

Keep Campfires Small and Safe. Conserve the area's firewood supply by collecting a limited amount, building a small campfire, and burning it for a short time. For example, a small fire would use wood up to 1.5 inches in diameter broken into 1-foot pieces, with a diameter less than 2 feet and flame height under 1 foot. Larger fires waste scarce wood and are more apt to damage nearby trees, kill tree roots, generate bothersome smoke and flying embers, become unsafe when windy, and produce larger quantities of ash and charcoal. Campfires must be located away from flammable ground litter like tree leaves and needles, dry vegetation, overhanging branches, tents, or other gear. If necessary, push organic litter a few feet back from the fire site. Never leave a campfire unattended, even for a few minutes—many forest fires have started from unattended campfires. If needed, bring a fire starter to help start your campfire— never use gas.

Burn All Wood to Ash and Extinguish with Water. Small-diameter firewood burns easily and completely to ash, reducing the accumulation of large mounds of charcoal in campfire rings. Charcoal can also be reduced

Campfires are *not* trash cans. Burning trash and food completely is not possible. It also attracts dangerous wildlife to campsites, creates noxious fumes, and leaves behind hazardous chemicals from plastic and the dyes found in paper. JEFFREY MARION

by not adding new fuel to a fire near the end of its use and by tending it, tossing in all the burned ends of wood. Allow all wood and coals to burn to white ash before putting it out when you have the time and it's safe (e.g., people present, little wind, no nearby flammable materials). To extinguish a campfire, saturate all areas of the fire site with plenty of water, stir the remains, add more water, and stir again. Feel all materials with your hands to ensure they are cool and *dead out*. Make sure that no coals, roots, or duff are burning and never bury your coals—they can smolder for days and erupt into flames when no one is around.

Leave a Clean Campfire Site. On developed or established campsites where campfires are legal, leave a clean fire ring for the campers that follow by removing and packing out any trash. In frontcountry, place the extinguished ashes in a trash bag to take home for disposal, or put in a trash container. In backcountry, widely scatter the *completely extinguished* ashes and charcoal in areas away from campsites. If time permits, consider removing all traces of illegal fire sites or of multiple fire sites, leaving only the one that best preserves tenting areas and is away from trees and roots. Check with land managers for guidance when in doubt. Consider reconstructing rock campfire sites to a diameter of about 3 feet to encourage small campfires and widely scattering any unnecessary rocks. Leave leftover firewood in one neat stack—dispersing it entails further off-site traffic by you and future campers to collect it again. When dispersed or "pristine site" camping, you should remove all traces of campfire sites. Widely scatter all cold ashes, charcoal, and firewood, return any excavated soils to their original location, and naturalize the site to remove all evidence of the campfire.

Respect Wildlife

Observe wildlife from a distance. If they react to your presence, you are too close. Never allow wildlife to obtain any human food—it is unhealthy for them, leads to attraction and nuisance behaviors, and creates dangerous dependencies.

Opportunities to encounter and view wildlife are often an important part of high-quality outdoor experiences. Unfortunately, wildlife face threats from loss and fragmentation of habitat, invasive species, pollution, overexploitation, poaching, and disease. Protected lands offer a last refuge from some, but not all, of these problems.

Studies show that animals respond to people in different ways. Some species adapt readily to humans in their domain, resume their normal behaviors, and are said to be "habituated." Other animals flee from humans, abandoning their young or critical habitat. Still others are attracted to and endangered by human food and trash.

Wild animals need recreationists who will promote their survival rather than add to the difficulties they already face. Because outdoor recreation is dispersed over large areas and at all times of the year, its impacts on wildlife can be equally extensive. Fish, birds, mammals, and reptiles are affected by people using their habitats. You can help by adopting behaviors that allow you to coexist peacefully with wildlife.

Observe from a Distance

Always watch or photograph animals from a safe distance to avoid startling them or forcing them to flee. Do not follow or approach wildlife.

Whether you are fishing, hunting, hiking, or picnicking, respecting wildlife is always important. Follow local game and fish laws and specific recommendations for minimizing your impact on area wildlife. BEN LAWHON

Avoid loud or startling noises, quick movements, and direct eye contact, which may be interpreted as aggression. Stalking or disturbing wildlife to view or photograph them forces animals to expend energy unnecessarily and moves them away from the best habitats. Consider the substantial impacts to wildlife if every visitor did that. If animals are on the move, stay out of their line of travel when possible. Except in bear country, travel quietly—you'll see more wildlife. Use the observation areas, platforms, and trails provided in many areas, and bring binoculars, spotting scopes, and telephoto lenses to watch or photograph wildlife from a distance. Back away if animals react to your presence. To leave the area, move away from the animal even if you must detour from your intended travel direction. You have more options in your movements than animals do. Treat them with due consideration and respect—*remember you are a visitor in* their *home.*

Do not encircle or crowd wildlife, harrass them, or attempt to catch or pick up a wild animal (most animals will bite or kick). Habituated wildlife may appear safe and non-threatening but keep a safe distance and remember that they are unpredictable *wild* animals. Dangerous incidents occur every year in parks when these presumed "safe" animals suddenly turn on visitors, resulting in injuries and even fatalities. Young animals may be aggressively protected by their parents, or abandoned if they or the nest/den site has a human scent. Notify a game warden if you find an animal in trouble. Show respect and restraint by teaching children not to approach, catch, or feed wild animals. Always keep children in immediate sight in areas with large predators, as they are often the same size as animal prey.

Avoid Sensitive Times and Habitats. Animals are more sensitive to recreationists while pursuing and defending mates and territories, birthing, guarding young or nests/dens, when food is scarce, and during cold or inclement weather. The more you understand about wildlife and a particular species, the more considerate you can be of the animal's needs and temperament, especially at critical times or places. For example, camping near the only water source for miles around in arid areas can prevent wildlife from accessing water during your stay. Consider the seasonal stresses that wildlife face. Songbirds are wary of humans and trails when choosing nesting territories in the spring. Wintertime disturbance of bats by cavers can interrupt hibernation and decrease their chance of survival. Bears frequent berry patches in late summer that also attract hikers. Be particularly aware of disturbing wildlife during sensitive times and avoid their habitats for your safety and theirs.

Never Feed Wild Animals

Animals are adept opportunists. When tempted by easy food offered by a visitor, or attracted to dropped or unattended food or trash, they can overcome their natural wariness of humans. Animals that obtain human food frequently develop dangerous food attraction behaviors and dependencies, turning them into aggressive beggars that can threaten human safety and property. Numerous serious and fatal human injuries have occurred from bears seeking human food. Extra precautions are important when visiting bear country (see page 68). Bites from small food-conditioned animals like chipmunks and mice are common injuries, and bites or close contact with them can transmit deadly diseases such as rabies and hantavirus.

Observe wildlife quietly from a distance with binoculars or telephoto lenses. You are too close if an animal stops its normal activities or moves away. Also, safely storing your food and trash from wildlife is essential to avoid creating dangerous food attraction behaviors that turn wildlife into beggars. Human food is unhealthy for wildlife. JEFFREY MARION

In conflicts with humans, animals ultimately lose, as suggested by the phrase, "a fed bear is a dead bear." Prospects of an easy meal also lure wildlife into hazardous locales such as campgrounds, trailheads, and roads, where they may be chased by dogs, hit by vehicles, or exposed to predators. They may also congregate in unnatural numbers, increasing stress and the spread of disease within their populations. Food-attracted wildlife suffer nutritionally, become dependent on unreliable human food sources, and condemn their young to a similar fate because they aren't taught how to find natural foods.

On hikes or when picnicking and camping accept responsibility to keep wildlife wild by not allowing them to obtain *any* human food or trash. This includes intentional feeding, food that you accidentally drop or spill, and food or trash in packs, on picnic tables, or stored at your campsite. Be aware that intentional and unintentional feeding of wildlife is strictly prohibited in most parks and wildlife refuges. Human food is generally not healthy for wildlife—potato chips are not on the "nutritious foods list" for deer, birds, or chipmunks! Research shows that wildlife live longer, healthier lives when they forage for their natural foods. It is important to note that food attraction behavior can develop even when the amounts of human food are small, such as a few dropped pieces of a granola bar or some spilled noodles (often termed "micro-garbage"). Mice that steal from your food supplies at night take up residence in camping shelters and cabins and can transmit the deadly hantavirus to humans. Even food smells can be a sufficient attractant, such as an unsecured trash bag containing only food wrappers and empty soda cans.

Store Food, Trash, and Smellables Securely. Wild animals are attracted not just to human, pet, or stock food but also to trash and other smellables, such as drink containers, dirty dishes, insect repellent, medicines, first-aid kits, lip balm, lotions, soaps, toothpaste, deodorant, and other toiletries. Anything with an interesting smell can attract wild animals, regardless of whether it's actually edible. Also note that wildlife have a substantially better sense of smell than humans do—bear's sense of smell has been calculated to be roughly two thousand times better than a human's! The specific animals of concern and safe methods for storing food, trash, and smellables vary considerably from place to place, so consult with local land managers and arrive prepared to store your food securely.

Serious illness or death can occur when wildlife get into your food when you aren't around. At Grand Canyon National Park, managers had to kill twenty-two food-attracted deer that became aggressive and dangerous. Autopsies revealed underweight and malnourished animals with up to 5 pounds of plastic and foil food packaging obstructing their intestines. The food wrappers were consumed from camping and picnic areas, often with food taken from unattended picnic tables and packs. Bears get the most attention for tearing into tents, coolers, and cars in search of a meal, but outdoor visitors more commonly have to deal with the annoyance of persistent rodents, raccoons, or skunks looking to score an easy meal from improperly stored items. When they adopt food attraction behaviors these animals can become a significant and dangerous nuisance to you, your gear, and other visitors.

Here are some universal "best practices" for food, trash, and smellables storage:

+ Keep trails and sites clean by removing all garbage and even the smallest scraps of food or trash.
+ Use wildlife-proof trash receptacles and food storage boxes whenever available.
+ Follow all precautions under the "Dispose of Waste Properly" (page 31) principle. For example, avoid or properly store and pack out all leftovers and kitchen waste, particularly bacon grease and cooking oils.
+ Never leave food for other visitors—wildlife will inevitably find and eat unattended food or drinks.
+ Store all food, trash, and smellables securely from wildlife during the day and at night. Outside of bear country, these items can be safely stored in vehicles or in heavy-duty plastic containers with clamped lids or straps. Always secure unattended coolers with straps. Five-gallon buckets with screw-on lids also make good trash and food storage containers.

Bear country. When camping in bear country, hang food, trash, and smellables from tree limbs 12 feet off the ground, 6 feet from any tree trunk or large limbs, and 6 feet below supporting limbs. Other alternatives include storage in specially designed bear-proof canisters or on-site lockers. Never underestimate the ingenuity or persistence of a bear! Vehicles do not protect your food from bears that have learned to pry back car

Properly storing food and trash in bear country is critical. Hanging bear bags can be challenging, and should be one of the first things you do upon arriving at camp. It is much easier to hang a bear bag in the daylight than at night. Bags should be hung 12 feet off the ground and 6 feet from the tree trunk and nearest branches. BEN LAWHON

Keeping your pet on a leash or otherwise in control is the best way to minimize its impact on local wildlife or other people. BEN LAWHON

windows or pop open trunks. Set up and store food, trash, and all smellables in suspended bear bags as soon as you arrive at your campsite, not just during the night. Take out items only when needed and for the minimum time necessary. Bear-proof backpacking canisters are available for rent and sale at sporting goods suppliers and some land management agencies. Used properly, they ensure a good night's sleep for you and a natural diet for bears.

For your safety, set up tents and hammocks at least 200 feet (80 steps) from cooking and dishwashing areas, don't take food or smellables into your tent, and change into clean clothes for sleeping. Clothing that smells of spilled food should be stored with your food. If a bear does visit your camp, yell loudly to scare it away and wake others up. You may need to group up and leave the campsite if the bear doesn't scare easily. Never approach or provoke a bear, even if it has some of your gear or food.

Control Your Pet

Pets and wildlife are rarely a good mix. Dogs and cats are domesticated predators that often retain natural prey-chasing and killing instincts. In some states, officials may capture and even dispose of dogs found running at large or chasing, injuring, or threatening wildlife or livestock. Your dog may also be injured by wildlife, vehicles, or horses, or have perilous encounters with porcupines, skunks, or leg-hold traps. Even leashed dogs can scare off wildlife and unleashed dogs may injure or kill wildlife, chase them for miles and become lost, or return full of porcupine quills. Sometimes the best option is to leave them at home. Obedience champion or not, every dog has the potential to bolt after fleeing wildlife before an owner can respond.

Pets are also potential carriers and recipients of wildlife diseases and parasites, often through their feces. If you do travel with your pet, check for any restrictions in advance. Ensure that your animal has current vaccinations for distemper, rabies, and parvovirus, and is parasite free (e.g., heartworm and other parasites).

Cats present different but equally significant problems. Recent research estimates that domestic cats in the United States kill 1.4 to 3.7 billion birds and 6.9 to 20.7 billion small mammals each year. In one study, a well-fed cat killed at least 60 birds and 1,600 small mammals in an 18-month period. Studies show that feeding, declawing, and putting bells on cats provide little deterrence—keeping them indoors is the only effective option. Additional information on managing your pet is included under the next principle (see page 77).

Be Considerate of Other Visitors

Respect is a simple concept: if you offer respect, you are more likely to receive it. Choose to act in ways that reduce the potential for crowding, conflicts, and unnecessary noise.

Visitation to protected areas continues to grow as surrounding lands are developed and human populations expand. Our protected areas are subject to increasing visitation and levels of crowding, particularly at popular attraction features and destinations. Recent decades have also seen a dramatic expansion in the diversity of recreation activities that visitors pursue in protected areas, including fast-moving wheeled and motorized activities that can be the source of additional conflict between recreationists. It's becoming increasingly important for visitors to share trails and recreation areas and adopt practices that sustain and improve the quality of everyone's outdoor experience. There is simply not enough space for every type of enthusiast to have exclusive use of trails, picnic areas, rivers, or campgrounds.

The subject of outdoor "etiquette" is often neglected. We're reluctant to examine our personal behaviors, least of all when recreating in the outdoors, where a sense of freedom is often paramount. Scientists suggest that it begins with our expanding diversity of recreational motives: some visitors are intent on improving their outdoor skills, others seek to escape their daily routines or find solitude, while others seek enjoyable outdoor adventures with family or friends. A canoeist or rock climber focused on improving his or her skills may achieve a high-quality experience despite some crowding or conflict with others. In contrast, a bird watcher's outdoor experience may be degraded by encountering even a few other visitors or any loud activity.

Step off-trail onto durable surfaces to allow horses or other trail users to pass. Move to the downhill side in steeper terrain. JEFFREY MARION

Respect Other Visitors and Protect the Quality of Their Experience

Our public lands must accommodate a wide range of recreational activities and levels of visitation. During your outdoor visits, accept the need for sharing public lands with other visitors, including those unlike yourself. Plan your trip carefully and guide your group to areas where you can achieve a high-quality experience while promoting equally high-quality experiences for other visitors that you encounter. Explore websites, ask knowledgeable friends, and contact land managers for information needed to plan a successful trip. Consider the types and amounts of use you are likely to encounter in different areas and times and plan your visit accordingly. A few "presumptions" may help to reduce the potential for crowding and conflicts with others:

- ✦ *Presume* that those you meet prefer to see and hear few other visitors. However, recognize that motives vary by environmental setting, activity, and type of visitor. If practical, plan your trip to avoid

Remember that all outdoor enthusiasts are trying to share a finite resource, and we all benefit from sharing trails, crags, rivers, and campgrounds. A kind word or deed can go a long way toward ensuring that all enjoy their time outside. BEN LAWHON

popular attraction features or trails during periods of high use. In backcountry or wilderness settings, choose a campsite that is out of sight of other visitors when possible or appropriate to do so. Visit with a smaller group or camp away from other sites. Refrain from yelling, loud talking, or other noises that may disturb nearby visitors, particularly in the evenings and at night.

✦ *Presume* that your chosen outdoor activity may conflict with the activity of some other groups of recreationists. Plan your activity to avoid areas where such conflicts may arise. Check for and follow land management type-of-use regulations or suggestions. For example, horses or mountain bikes may be restricted or recommended for certain trails, or motorized uses may be limited to certain areas.

✦ *Presume* that the motives and elements of a high-quality outdoor experience for other visitors are different from your own. Pay attention to the visitors you encounter and make an effort to discern how your group's activities and behaviors are affecting the quality of their experience. When in doubt, ask them. To the extent possible, alter your group's activity and behavior accordingly, and alter where or when you go on future trips.

Choose to maintain a cooperative spirit during outdoor activities. Our interactions should reflect the knowledge that we can and do rely on each other when mishaps occur. More often than not, our experiences ultimately depend on our treatment of others and their attitudes toward us. Although our motivations and sense of adventure vary, there's always room on the trail for people with open minds and generous hearts.

Share the Trail. The little things are often the most important. Simple courtesies such as offering a friendly greeting on the trail, using earthtoned clothing and gear to blend with the scenery, allowing others to pass, or preserving the natural quiet all make a difference. When taking a break, don't block the trail; continue until you find a good durable off-trail area large enough for your group.

Groups leading or riding livestock have the right of way on trails. Hikers and bicyclists should move to the downhill side and stop. Some horses spook easily when encountering dogs, small children, and people riding bicycles or wearing large backpacks, so greet and talk to riders as they approach to let horses know you're human. When encountering others on the trail yield to uphill traffic, slow down (be prepared to stop if necessary), greet them to announce your presence, and pass on the left in a safe and friendly manner. Avoid widening the trail by staying on it, or look for a durable surface on which to pass or pause. If you use earphones, keep the volume low or wear them in one ear so you can hear other trail users when they are attempting to pass you. When on bikes, stay in control and slow down on blind corners and when approaching others.

Respect Private Property and Native People. Private land is *not* open to public use without the landowner's permission. It is your responsibility to know whether land is private or public; private land boundaries may not be fenced or clearly marked with signs. If you are granted permission to use private land, preserve that opportunity for future visitors by taking extra precautions to Leave No Trace of your visit. Be friendly and courteous to the owners and be sure to thank them for letting you enjoy their property.

Local ranchers often have grazing or agricultural permits on public lands. Respect these uses by always leaving gates *as you find them*, open or

Always respect private property, and only enter with the permission of the landowner. Where permission is granted, leave things as good as or better than you found them.
LEAVE NO TRACE CENTER FOR OUTDOOR ETHICS

closed, and by not disturbing livestock, crops, or the equipment of loggers, miners, outfitters, or others.

Likewise, show your respect to native peoples whose communities and seasonal camps support a subsistence lifestyle. Be friendly, unobtrusive, and self-sufficient. Take note of tribal land boundaries, ask permission to cross their lands, and obey special laws and restrictions. Respect voluntary closures of public lands for Native American ceremonies.

Manage Your Pet. Check with the local land managers for regulations or guidance on bringing pets with you when visiting parks or forests. For example, most national parks prohibit dogs on trails, while other areas require the use of leashes. Show respect for other visitors and wildlife by keeping your pet under physical restraint, or consider leaving your pet at home. If it is permissible to bring your dog on a hike, it's best to use a leash and shorten it when encountering others. Allow your dog off leash only if permissible and when you are certain it poses no threat to other visitors or wildlife. At campsites or picnic areas, ask other visitors if it's OK for your dog to be off leash; monitor your dog to see that it does not bother or frighten other vistors, or get into their food or trash. Recognize that some people, particularly children, are frightened by all dogs and

People enjoy the outdoors in different ways. Do your part by respecting how others choose to spend time outside and allowing them the opportunity to experience solitude, silence, or natural sounds. BEN LAWHON

that your dog may not mix well with horses, mountain bikers, or other pets. Remove pet feces from trails, picnic areas, and campsites by disposing of it in an approved receptacle or trashcan, or in a cat-hole in backcountry settings (follow guidance in "Dispose of Waste Properly," page 31).

Let Nature's Sounds Prevail. Natural sounds, like the bugling of an elk in the mountains, can have a powerful effect on us and make visiting the outdoors a unique experience. However, human-related noise can intrude upon and easily overcome natural sounds. The discharge of firearms can be heard for miles, and car alarms, barking dogs, and vehicle engines, particularly motorcycles, are audible from almost as far. Car and portable music systems are also common forms of "noise pollution" in parks and forests. Minimize your "noise footprint," especially at night and in remote areas. Keep your voice low and encourage others to do the same, keep dogs quiet, and wear headphones to listen to music. Car campgrounds are particularly challenging because of the higher density of campers. Take extra care to minimize the unwanted sounds from electric generators, noisy campfire activity and late-night conversations, slamming vehicle and restroom doors, and vehicle engines or alarms. Remember to *tune in* to the sounds of nature!

While many outdoor recreationists carry cell phones for safety and emergencies, recognize that other visitors object to seeing and hearing your phone conversations in outdoor settings. Be considerate of other visitors by carrying and using cell phones discreetly, out of sight and sound of other people. Keep them turned off until needed or left in a pocket on the "vibrate" or "silent" setting. Similarly, avoid the use of radios, electronic games, and other intrusive devices around others. To some, technology is a necessity even in outdoor settings. To others, it is inappropriate. Avoid conflicts by making a conscious effort to be discreet in the use of technology when involved in outdoor activities.

LEAVE NO TRACE ETHICS

> "The nation behaves well if it treats natural resources as assets, which it must turn over to the next generation increased and not impaired in value." —Theodore Roosevelt

> "Be the change you wish to see in the world." —Gandhi

Early European settlers regarded the immense wilderness of the North American continent as both an asset to be developed and an obstacle to progress. The island remnants of that vast wilderness are today preserved primarily in our parks, forests, rangelands, and wildlife refuges. The human values of these protected areas expand as humankind increasingly modifies surrounding lands. However, these values are contingent on our collective ability to protect natural areas from external impacts, like air pollution and non-native species, and internal impacts, like degradation from visitor use.

Theodore Roosevelt, the noted conservation president, recognized the societal values of protecting our nation's natural resources when he created the National Wildlife Refuge system and signed legislation creating five national parks and eighteen national monuments. Over a century ago, he emphasized the ethical and stewardship obligations of protecting these public resources for the benefit of future generations. He recognized that merely designating such protected areas does not guarantee their preservation—that requires professional management actively supported by visitors who also apply the best available low-impact practices. The challenge of our generation and those that follow is to ensure

Ethics are often thought of as "what you do when no one is looking," and they are a crucial part of Leave No Trace. Outdoor ethics should guide your choices about recreating responsibly on every outing. BEN LAWHON

the continued protection of our rich natural and cultural heritage—including from our own recreational visits.

While Roosevelt's philosophy remains sound, the practices that are considered sustainable have changed as our population has grown and we have gained new knowledge about ecology and ecosystem processes. Technological advances in outdoor gear also allow us to carry lightweight tents or hammocks that remain dry without ditching, and to substitute stoves for higher-impact campfires, or sleeping pads for beds of cut boughs, grasses, or moss. Such gear can substantially reduce resource impacts and provide greater efficiency, safety, and comfort, though the environmental impacts of their manufacturing and shipping represent trade-offs to be considered.

We *can* enjoy protected areas without harming them—but only if we assume a personal responsibility to learn about and apply the best available low-impact practices, and share our knowledge and skills with others. Remember that we are visitors; we must behave in a manner that is

Passing along outdoor ethics to the next generation is imperative. Help children learn about Leave No Trace skills and ethics, and teach them how to be good stewards of the outdoors. BEN LAWHON

respectful of the animals and plants that live there. Consider the consequences of your actions in light of the question: What if everyone did this? The Leave No Trace program teaches the ethics and practical skills to help fulfill our collective responsibility to Leave No Trace of our outdoor visits. As Gandhi teaches us, *we can be the catalyst for changing others* and the world around us. Educate yourself about Leave No Trace, take a Leave No Trace Trainer or Master Educator course, and then teach others! Leave No Trace is *everyone's* responsibility.

What Compels Us to Do the Right Thing? Is it a government agency's regulations or the threat of their enforcement? Are we simply following a set of rules specifying "dos" and "don'ts," or the guidance of a parent or outdoor leader? Or is it a personal ethical response compelling us to act in ways that protect the outdoor environments that we love to visit? Ethics are moral principles that define right from wrong; behaviors guided by ethics are freely chosen and self-directed, and any behavioral constraints are self-imposed. *Ethics govern what we do when no one's* *looking.* Our success in voluntarily avoiding and minimizing the impacts of our visits helps reduce the need for managers to limit visitation or enact regulations restricting our behaviors.

The seven principles of Leave No Trace provide a framework of principled behavior that can serve as a basis for ecologically responsible interactions with natural environments. Leave No Trace ethics apply not just during backcountry visits but also to outdoor recreation pursuits near your home and in everyday living. All outdoor environments, regardless of their level of development and naturalness, can benefit when visitors adopt low-impact practices. When camping we choose to protect trees by not bringing an ax or saw, instead using downed firewood we can break by hand. Our respect for wildlife causes us to store our food and trash out of their reach and to observe them from a distance. We resist the urge to pick a flower, knowing that would deny other visitors the opportunity to see it, or the plant its ability to produce seeds and new plants.

Learn about nature if you really want to protect it. An enhanced understanding of natural environments and processes will improve your ability to judge the consequences of alternative outdoor practices. What are the best available durable surfaces? Should you choose a well-established trail or campsite or disperse your activity? Consider the many options relating to campfires, from substituting a gas stove or charcoal grill, to a fire ring or a mound or pit fire. Choosing the best low-impact practice requires knowledge of the environment around you, your activity and type of group, land manager guidance, weather conditions, and your low-impact knowledge and skills. Your choices will have profound effects on the environment around you and the experiences of other visitors.

Apply the 3 R's—Reduce, Reuse, and Recycle—when recreating and in your everyday life. Check local thrift and second-hand stores for used outdoor clothing and gear and donate your unused items to stores for reuse. Consider making your own clothing or gear. Cut your carbon footprint by carpooling or using public transportation options for outdoor visits and trips. Combine recreation and exercise for transportation by walking or biking to the local park or work. Do some online investigation and make informed choices to purchase the most "green" eco-friendly products possible. Consider how Leave No Trace ethics apply to your home and work life. Challenge yourself to live more sustainably!

LEAVE NO TRACE IN THE FRONTCOUNTRY

rontcountry includes outdoor areas that are easily accessible by vehicle and mostly visited by day users, including protected areas close to home and the developed portions of traditional parks and forests. Frontcountry practices may differ from those applied in more remote settings, primarily due to site developments and facilities and differences in recreation activities and equipment. Here are some examples:

Stick to Trails. Traveling on trails leaves room for wildlife and their homes. Short-cutting trails causes erosion. Be ready to get muddy and step right through puddles. Boots dry overnight; plants take years to recover.

Protect Our Waters. Riparian areas are vital to the health and diversity of animal and plant life. These areas are often the sole habitat for many plant and animal species that need wet conditions.

Manage Your Dog. Keeping your dog in control keeps people, other pets, livestock, and wildlife safe. Others may not appreciate your dog's company, so ask before allowing your dog to approach them. Keep your dog nearby and under control. Carry and use a leash as required.

Respect Private Property. Respect "No Trespassing" signs. If property boundaries are unclear, do not enter the area. Treat another's property as you would treat your own.

Pick Up Poop. Phew! Dog poop stinks and others can step in it. Pack a bag and always pick up your dog's poop—wherever it's left.

Keep Wildlife Wild. Natural areas are home to wildlife. As a visitor, you should respect wildlife by observing them from a distance and not feeding them.

Trash Your Trash. Please take out all trash, both yours and that of others. Even "biodegradable" materials such as orange peels, apple cores,

Frontcountry areas such as this are often heavily visited and sometimes heavily impacted. Choose frontcountry sites that are well suited to your needs and learn about ways to minimize your impacts while visiting these places. BEN LAWHON

and food scraps can take years to break down, and they attract scavengers that harm other wildlife.

Leave It as You Find It. Picking flowers, collecting rocks, or taking arrowheads may not seem like a big deal, but it means others won't have a chance to enjoy them. With millions of recreationists, the less impact each of us makes, the longer we will enjoy what we have.

Share Our Trails. We all enjoy the outdoors in different ways. Pay attention, expect to encounter others, and be courteous.

A FINAL CHALLENGE

Contact land management agencies and groups in your area to learn how you can help. Be an active participant and collaborator in the planning and management of areas that are important to you. Volunteer for clean-up or invasive plant control efforts, trail maintenance, and rehabilitation projects, or organize them for your local area. Become a "citizen scientist" and volunteer to monitor resource conditions or carry out stewardship projects. Get involved and let your opinions on land use be known. Develop your low-impact knowledge and teach a Leave No Trace course. Accept the challenge to get involved and make a difference.

Information on obtaining Leave No Trace curriculum materials, courses, and trainings is available by calling 800-332-4100 or by visiting the Leave No Trace website: www.LNT.org.

Another resource for visitors using motorized or mechanized craft or vehicles is the Tread Lightly program. Contact Tread Lightly, Inc. at 800-966-9900 or visit their website: www.treadlightly.org.

Stay on formal trails to avoid creating informal (visitor-created) trails that unnecessarily impact adjacent vegetation and soils. Walk single file on barren substrates to avoid widening trails. JEFFREY MARION

RESOURCES

Leave No Trace
Courses

A variety of formal Leave No Trace courses are available to provide additional education on Leave No Trace outdoor skills and ethics. Shorter Awareness Workshops and the Online Awareness course present an introductory overview of Leave No Trace skills and ethics for outdoor enthusiasts of all types. The Master Educator (5-day) and Trainer (2-day) courses provide more comprehensive experiential training and are designed for outdoor educators and others interested in more advanced knowledge. Visit the Leave No Trace website to search for Master Educator or Trainer courses offered near you. Pick the training that's best for you!

Online Awareness Course. This 1-hour course highlights the principles of Leave No Trace and provides a brief overview of low-impact practices and ethics.

Awareness Workshops. These 1-hour to 1-day introductory workshops introduce you to the seven principles of Leave No Trace and cover the core low-impact practices. Workshops are designed for groups of outdoor enthusiasts, including youth camps, college students, outdoor professionals, Girl or Boy Scouts, and hiking club members.

Trainer Course. This 2-day experiential course, taught by one or more Master Educators, assists participants in learning more in-depth knowledge about Leave No Trace practices and ethics, and techniques for disseminating low-impact skills. Trainer Courses are designed for outdoor educators, trip leaders from camps, clubs, troops, or colleges, guides, agency employees, and other outdoor professionals. Graduates of the Trainer Course gain skills to teach Leave No Trace practices to their family, friends, and clients in a variety of settings.

Author Jeff Marion, crouching in center, with members of his Venture Crew following a caving trip in the Virginia Mountains. LEAVE NO TRACE CENTER FOR OUTDOOR ETHICS

Master Educator Course. This 5-day experiential learning course provides participants with comprehensive training in Leave No Trace skills and ethics through practical application in a field-based setting. Offered by a restricted number of authorized organizations, each course is staffed with a minimum of two highly experienced outdoor professionals. The first day is spent in a classroom, where the course and schedule are introduced along with in-depth information on several aspects of the Leave No Trace program. The remaining four days are spent hiking, riding, or paddling in the field, learning and practicing the principles of Leave No Trace. You will learn low-impact practices through skits, discussions, and hands-on activities. To practice Leave No Trace teaching strategies in a supportive, educational environment, each participant teaches a short session on one of the principles. Successful graduates become Master Educators authorized to teach Leave No Trace Trainer Courses. As of January 2014, there were over 6,000 Leave No Trace Master Educators worldwide, representing 40 countries and the 50 United States.

Skills & Ethics Booklet Series

For additional Leave No Trace information on low-impact practices tailored to specific outdoor activities or environmental settings, purchase Skills & Ethics booklets (20–30 pages) at LNT.org/shop/publications.

Leave No Trace has been adapted for many environments, activities, and ecosystems. Regardless of how you choose to spend time outdoors, there is Leave No Trace information that is just right for you. LEAVE NO TRACE CENTER FOR OUTDOOR ETHICS

Specialized Outdoor Activities

Caving
Mountain Biking
Rock Climbing
Sea Kayaking
Horse Use
Fishing

Environmental Settings

Alaskan Tundra
Rocky Mountains
Deserts and Canyons
Sierra Nevada
Lakes Region
Southeast
North America
Western River Corridors
Northeast Mountains
Pacific Northwest

Leave No Trace for Groups

Organized groups provide outdoor training, equipment, expertise, and logistical support for everyone from novices looking for an adventure to experts seeking a unique experience with the help of a guide. Group trips into the outdoors play a critical role in shaping the lifelong skills and ethics of their participants. Many outdoor enthusiasts are introduced to the outdoors on a scouting trip, a church group overnight, at a summer camp, or through a hiking club or school field

Regardless of the kind of activity, the environment, or the size of the group, all groups must learn about outdoor ethics and practice Leave No Trace when outdoors.
DEAN RONZONI

trip. For this reason, groups are integral to getting Leave No Trace information out to a wide and diverse audience.

However, large organized groups in the outdoors sometimes earn a bad reputation. Noise, crowding, trash, poor sanitation, trampling, and undue impacts on the land are often blamed on large groups. Sometimes these labels are deserved; more often they are not. Current research indicates that the techniques a group uses and how it behaves in the outdoors are more important than its size in determining how the group will affect the land and other visitors.

Leave No Trace has developed a pamphlet designed to help your group develop and adopt Leave No Trace practices that preserve both our outdoor resources and the quality of outdoor experiences. It is intended to complement the more in-depth guidance provided by this book, Leave No Trace courses, and the Leave No Trace Skills & Ethics booklet series. Your success in instilling these ethics in your group will make a significant difference in the condition of the outdoors and the recreational experience we all enjoy there. It may also prevent further regulations or group size limitations from being imposed. Make Leave No Trace a core part of your group's agenda and help protect the places we cherish.

Please download and share the Leave No Trace for Groups pamphlet: LNT.org/sites/default/files/GroupUseBrochure.pdf

Suggestion: Share this file via e-mail with adult and youth leaders participating on each outing.

A Brief History of the
Leave No Trace Program

L and managers face a perennial struggle in their efforts to achieve an appropriate balance between the competing mandates to preserve natural and cultural resources and provide high-quality recreational opportunities. Visitor education designed to instill low-impact skills and ethics is a critical management component and is seen as a light-handed approach that can reduce the need for more direct and regulatory forms of management.

Low-impact educational programs were originally developed by the U.S. federal land management agencies in response to substantial increases in outdoor recreation in the late 1960s. For example, National Park Service visitation more than doubled from 1960 to 1970 (72 to 170 million), while U.S. Forest Service visitation to backcountry and wilderness areas tripled during this period. Media coverage on this surge in outdoor recreation began to question if Americans were "loving their parks to death," and land managers witnessed a range of associated resource impacts including proliferation of visitor-created campsites and trails, litter, tree damage, and the loss of vegetation and soil. They responded to this environmental degradation by implementing new regulations and educational messages. Most land managers operate under congressional laws directing them to provide for recreational visitation while preserving natural conditions and processes. These legal mandates became increasingly challenging when visitation was high, or when resource protection guidance was strong, such as for designated wilderness areas.

Land managers initially turned to regulations, but as noted by Jim Bradley, a Forest Service wilderness specialist, a purely regulatory approach is inappropriate because:

 ✦ regulations antagonize the public rather than win their support,
 ✦ most impacts are from a lack of knowledge regarding appropriate low-impact practices, not from malicious acts, and
 ✦ enforcement of regulations is difficult in wildlands because of their large and remote nature.

Instead, land managers began developing educational programs to promote awareness of recreation impacts and to encourage visitors to voluntarily learn and apply low-impact practices that avoid or minimize such impacts. The federal agencies, notably the U.S. Forest Service (USFS), but also the Bureau of Land Management (BLM) and the National Park Service (NPS), developed numerous brochures during the 1970s and 1980s variously called "Wilderness Manners," "Wilderness Ethics," "Minimum Impact Camping," and "No-Trace Camping."

> Wilderness management is 80–90 percent education and information and 10 percent regulation.
> —Max Peterson, former Chief of the U.S. Forest Service, 1985

These educational efforts originated largely in USFS Wilderness management programs in the Pacific Northwest. Wilderness Information Specialists were employed to engage visitors at agency offices, visitor centers, and trailheads, using a friendly approach to provide information on minimum-impact travel and camping practices. By the early 1980s a more formal "No-Trace" program emerged that cultivated new wilderness ethics and more sustainable low-impact outdoor practices. This program's success led to interagency coordination and in 1987 the USFS, NPS, and BLM cooperatively developed and distributed a pamphlet titled "Leave No Trace Land Ethics." Mirroring these efforts was the publication of a number of books describing appropriate low-impact practices, including "The Wilderness Handbook" (1974), the Sierra Club's "Walking Softly in the Wilderness" (1977), "Backwoods Ethics: Environmental Concerns for Hikers and Campers" (1979), and "Soft Paths" (1988). Research studies describing visitor impacts, influential factors, and low-impact practices also grew in number, forming the new "recreation ecology" field of study.

By 1990, the clear need for visitor education, coupled with increasing knowledge about visitor impacts from research, prompted the USFS to approach the National Outdoor Leadership School (NOLS) to assist in the further development of low-impact practices and training. NOLS was a recognized leader in developing and teaching wilderness skills, including low-impact hiking and camping practices. The intent was to develop a national program similar to the successful Smokey Bear (forest fire) and Woodsy Owl (litter) campaigns, and the Tread Lightly program initiated in 1985 to promote low-impact practices for motorized recreationists (www.treadlightly.org). A formal agreement was signed between USFS and NOLS in 1991, the same year it developed and taught the first five-day Master Educator course.

> "We have long recognized education as the best strategy for reversing the trend of damage to wilderness and undeveloped areas caused by recreation visitors ... Accordingly, the Forest Service developed and has actively sponsored Leave No Trace as our outdoor ethics program for non-motorized users."   —Dale Robertson, former Chief of the U.S. Forest Service, 1992

An expanded agreement was enacted in 1994 between NOLS and the USFS, NPS, BLM, and U.S. Fish & Wildlife Service, committing the federal agencies to provide overall direction for the national program, with NOLS supplying curricula, training, and the development and distribution of Leave No Trace information. NOLS produced and sold brochures, Skills & Ethics booklets, videos, and other educational materials via a toll-free number and website. Further program expansion required additional funding and support from outdoor product manufacturers and retailers and other outdoor organizations. Accordingly, in 1994, Leave No Trace, Inc., a nonprofit organization, was formed with the support of agency, commercial, and nonprofit partners. By 1996, the new organization had two full-time staff, a budget of $108,425, and a Board of Directors with eight members.

The national Leave No Trace program has continued to grow and expand, with the following milestones:

+ 1999—Leave No Trace principles revised to include a focus on protecting wildlife and visitor experiences; the Appalachian Mountain Club (AMC) was added as a new training partner for Master Educator courses.

+ 2000—nine full-time staff; completion of the sixteenth Skills & Ethics booklet on Leave No Trace practices.

+ 2001—1,122 Master Educators trained, including USFS (254), BLM (121), NPS (107), and USFWS (4).

+ 2002—Promoting Environmental Awareness in Kids (PEAK) program launched. The PEAK Program teaches youth ages six to twelve about Leave No Trace through fun and interactive activities.

+ 2003—official name changed to the Leave No Trace Center for Outdoor Ethics.

+ 2005—in addition to NOLS and AMC, Landmark Learning, the Wilderness Education Association, the Boy Scouts of America, and the USFS Ninemile Training Center were added as training partners for Master Educator courses.

+ 2006—a Frontcountry Leave No Trace educational outreach initiative was launched.

+ 2013—twelve full-time staff, 4 Leave No Trace/Subaru Traveling Trainer Teams, 6,000 Master Educators, and 30,000 Trainers.

The Center has branches outside the United States, too. Some practices differ, so check their websites for more information.

Leave No Trace Ireland: www.leavenotraceireland.org

Leave No Trace/Sans Trace Canada:
www.leavenotrace.ca/home

Glossary

Avoidable impact. Degradation such as tree damage or wildlife feeding that can be *completely avoided* without compromising the quality of recreational experiences. *Unavoidable impacts,* like trampling damage, can be minimized by adopting the best available low-impact practices.

Cairns. Stacks of rocks used to mark trails and guide hikers in treeless or trail-less areas. Creating new cairns or altering existing cairns can expand trampling impacts in sensitive environments or misdirect visitors into dangerous areas.

Concentration. Minimize impacts from trampling by concentrating traffic in popular areas and on formal or well-established trails and sites or on highly durable surfaces.

Dispersal. In more remote areas, disperse your traffic and activities to levels that prevent the formation of trails and sites. Avoid trampling plants and move to a new campsite or area if you see plant damage beginning to occur.

Durable surfaces. Pavement, rock, gravel, snow or ice, and barren soils that show little evidence of trampling. If durable surfaces are unavailable use non-vegetated areas of organic litter (leaves, pine needles) or dry grassy areas.

Formal and well-established trails and recreation sites. Designated or well-used trails, day-use sites, and campsites that land managers encourage using to contain trampling impacts on resistant surfaces designed and managed to sustain heavy traffic.

Frontcountry. Outdoor areas that are easily accessible by vehicle and mostly visited by day users, including protected areas close to home and the developed portions of traditional parks and forests.

Graywater. Water used in cooking or cleaning dishes; it may contain food particles or strong smells that attract wildlife, and it requires filtering and proper disposal.

Informal trails and recreation sites. Visitor-created trails, day-use sites, and campsites that land managers generally discourage visitors from using. Many are not sustainably designed, unnecessary, and could be avoided if visitors stayed on formal or well-established trails and sites, or dispersed their traffic to prevent their formation.

Naturalize. Removing all traces of your dispersed campsite or fire site by scattering rocks and woody debris and fluffing up organic litter and vegetation so that visitors will not be attracted to reusing that site.

Non-native plants and animals. Species that were not originally indigenous (native) to a particular area, i.e., they were transported into and introduced to an area. Non-native species that outcompete and replace native species and cause substantial ecological disruption and/or economic harm are often labeled as "invasive" species.

Popular areas. The more heavily visited portions of protected areas, including areas with attraction features and high-use destinations. You can minimize impact by concentrating use on formal or well-established trails and recreation sites.

Pristine areas. The less-visited, often remote, portions of protected areas. Impacts are best minimized by dispersing use so that trails and recreation sites never form, and by staying away from existing lightly impacted trails and sites to promote their recovery.

Smellables. Food, drink containers, trash, dirty dishes, insect repellent, medicines, first-aid kits, lip balm, lotions, soaps, toothpaste, deodorant, and other toiletries. Anything with an interesting smell can attract wild animals, regardless of whether it's actually edible.

Toilet types. *Flush toilets* transfer wastes to a sewage treatment plant or a nearby underground drain field. *Vault toilets* have a holding tank and wastes are periodically pumped out for disposal at sewage treatment plants. *Composting toilets* allow heat, worms, and microbes to naturally compost and break down the wastes. *Pit toilets* are dug directly in the earth and the toilet is moved and the pit filled in when full. *Portable toilets, bag systems,* and *poop tubes* temporarily contain wastes for disposal into flush toilets or a sewage disposal facility. Some require the use of chemical and enzyme products that allow the waste to be deposited in the trash for landfill disposal.

Trash-free or zero-waste events. Outings and group gatherings where participants bring food and drinks in reusable or recyclable containers to avoid, or substantially minimize, the amount of trash that must be carried out. Zero-waste events extend application to human waste and graywater disposal.

Wildlife habituation and attraction behavior. Habituated wildlife have learned to tolerate the presence of humans with limited impact. Animals that have obtained human food and trash develop food-attraction behaviors that can make them aggressive panhandlers. These animals become a dangerous nuisance and when they threaten human property or lives land managers sometimes have to kill them.

Further Reading

This book was developed based on the best available information from scientific research, outdoor organizations, land management agencies, and outdoor recreational experiences. It was reviewed and approved by the Leave No Trace Center for Outdoor Ethics and its Educational Review Committee, and by the U.S. Geological Survey peer-review program. The following reading list, organized by book sections, references much of the scientific and technical information this book was derived from and can be sought by readers for additional information. While many of these references can be located online through web searches, readers are also encouraged to search for other web-based information. The number of website addresses in the following list is limited because website addresses and materials frequently change.

Introduction

Brame, Rich, and David Cole. 2011. *NOLS Soft Paths*, 4th ed. Stackpole Books, Mechanicsburg, PA.

Cole, David. 2002. "Ecological impacts of wilderness recreation and management." In *Wilderness management: stewardship and protection of resources and values*. J. Hendee and C. Dawson. Fulcrum Publishing, Golden, CO. 413–59.

Cole, David N. 2004. "Impacts of hiking and camping on soils and vegetation: a review." In Ralf Buckley, ed. *Environmental impacts of ecotourism*. CAB International, Wallingford, UK. 41–60.

Cordell, Ken. 2012. "Outdoor Recreation Trends and Futures." USDA Forest Service, Southern Research Station, Asheville, NC.

Gutzwiller, Kevin, and David Cole. 2005. "Assessment and management of wildland recreational disturbance." In Clait Braun, ed. *Wildlife Management Techniques Manual*, 6th ed. The Wildlife Society, Bethesda, MD. 779–96.

Ham, Sam, Terry Brown, Jim Curtis, Betty Weiler, Michael Hughes, and Mark Poll. 2007. "Promoting persuasion in protected areas: A guide for managers." Sustainable Tourism CRC. Gold Coast, Queensland, Australia.

Hammitt, William, and David Cole. 1998. *Wildland Recreation: Ecology and Management*, 2nd ed. John Wiley & Sons, Inc., New York.

Leave No Trace Center for Outdoor Ethics. 2012. Leave No Trace website, www.LNT.org.

Leopold, Aldo. 1949. *A Sand County Almanac*. Oxford University Press, Inc., New York.

Leung, Yu-Fai, and Jeffrey Marion. 2000. "Recreation impacts and management in wilderness: A state-of-knowledge review." In *Proceedings: Wilderness Science in a Time of Change, 1999; Vol. 5: Wilderness ecosystems, threats, and management*, 23-48; Missoula, MT. Proceedings RMRS-P-15-Vol-5. USDA Forest Service, Rocky Mountain Research Station, Ogden, UT.

Manning, Robert. 2007. *Parks and carrying capacity: Commons without tragedy*. Island Press, Washington, DC.

———. 2003. "Emerging principles for using information/education in wilderness management." *International Journal of Wilderness* 9(1):20–27.

Marion, Jeffrey, and David Bates. 2005. "Implementing Leave No Trace at camps." American Camping Association, *Camping Magazine* 78(3):54–57.

Marion, Jeffrey, and Scott Reid. 2007. "Minimising visitor impacts to protected areas: The efficacy of low impact education programmes." *Journal of Sustainable Tourism* 15(1):5–27.

McGivney, Annette. 2003. *Leave No Trace: A guide to the new wilderness etiquette*. 2nd ed. The Mountaineers, Seattle, WA.

Newsome, David, Susan Moore, and Ross Dowling. 2002. *Natural area tourism: Ecology, impacts, and management*. Channel View Publications, Clevedon, UK.

Turner, James. 2002. "From Woodcraft to 'Leave No Trace': Wilderness, consumerism, and environmentalism in twentieth-century America." *Environmental History* 7(3):462–84.

Plan Ahead and Prepare

Cole, David N. 1989. "Low-impact recreational practices for wilderness and backcountry." USDA Forest Service, General Technical Report INT-265.

Eunomia Research and Consulting. 2008. "Guideline for working towards zero waste events." Auckland City Council, Auckland, New Zealand.

Leave No Trace Center for Outdoor Ethics. The Leave No Trace Skills & Ethics booklet series consists of 20–30 page booklets that provide in-depth descriptions of low-impact practices for a diverse range of recreational settings and outdoor activities, including Alaska Wildlands, Caving, Deserts and Camping, Fishing, Horse Use, Lakes Region, Mountain Biking, North America, Northeast Mountains, Pacific Northwest, Rock Climbing, Rocky Mountains, Sea Kayaking, Sierra Nevada, Southeast, and Western River Corridors.

Leave No Trace Center for Outdoor Ethics. Leave No Trace Courses. *Master Educator Course*—in-depth low-impact outdoor skills training (5 days) designed for people who actively teach others. *Trainer Course*—in-depth low-impact outdoor skills training (2 days) designed for group/trip leaders and other interested individuals. *Awareness Workshop*—low-impact outdoor skill instruction (<1 day) for all outdoor recreationists.

Leave No Trace Center for Outdoor Ethics. 2008. "Leave No Trace group use" brochure.

Leave No Trace Center for Outdoor Ethics. 2007. *Leave No Trace 101: 101 ways to teach Leave No Trace.* Boulder, CO.

London Organizing Committee of the Olympic Games and Paralympic Games Limited. 2012. London 2012 Zero-Waste Events Protocol. www.london2012.com.

Marion, Jeffrey, Teresa Martinez, and Robert Proudman. 2001. "Trekking poles: Can you save your knees and the environment?" *The Register* 24(5):1, 10, 11.

Martin, Steven, and Kate McCurdy. 2010. "Wilderness food storage: Are bear-resistant food storage canisters effective?" *International Journal of Wilderness* 16(1):13–19.

Monz, Christopher, Joseph Roggenbuck, David Cole, Richard Brame, and Andrew Yoder. 2000. "Wilderness party size regulations: implications for management and a decision-making framework." In David Cole, Stephen McCool, William Borrie, and Jennifer O'Loughlin, comps. *Wilderness science in a time of change conference. Vol. 4: Wilderness visitors, experiences, and visitor management.* USDA Forest Service Gen. Tech. Rep. RMRS-P-15-VOL-4:265–273.

USDA. 2010. "Risk assessment of the movement of firewood within the United States." U.S. Department of Agriculture, Animal and Plant Health Inspection Service, Raleigh, NC.

Travel and Camp on Durable Surfaces

Belnap, Jayne. 2003. "The world at your feet: Desert biological soil crusts." *Frontiers in Ecology and the Environment* 1(5):181–89.

Cole, David. 1989. "Low-impact recreational practices for wilderness and back-country." USDA Forest Service, General Technical Report INT-265.

———. 1990. "Trampling disturbance and recovery of cryptogamic soil crusts in Grand Canyon National Park." *Great Basin Naturalist* 20:321–26.

———. 1993. "Trampling effects on mountain vegetation in Washington, Colorado, New Hampshire, and North Carolina." USDA Forest Service Res. Pap. INT-464.

———. 1995. "Disturbance of natural vegetation by camping: Experimental applications of low-level stress." *Environmental Management* 19:405–16.

———. 1995. "Experimental trampling of vegetation. I. Relationship between trampling intensity and vegetation response." *Journal of Applied Ecology* 32:203–14.

Cole, David, and Chris Monz. 2003. "Impacts of camping on vegetation: Response and recovery following acute and chronic disturbance." *Environmental Management* 32(6):693–705.

Hockett, Karen, Amanda Clark, Yu-Fai Leung, Jeffrey Marion, and Logan Park. 2010. "Deterring off-trail hiking in protected natural areas: Evaluating options with surveys and unobtrusive observation." Virginia Tech College of Natural Resources & Environment, Blacksburg, VA.

Kuntz, Kathryn, and Douglas Larson. 2006. "Influences of microhabitat constraints and rock-climbing disturbance on cliff-face vegetation communities." *Conservation Biology* 20(3): 821–32.

Leung, Yu-Fai, and Jeffrey L. Marion. 1996. "Trail degradation as influenced by environmental factors: A state-of-the-knowledge review." *Journal of Soil and Water Conservation* 51(2):130–36.

Leung, Yu-Fai, and Jeffrey Marion. 2000. "Recreation impacts and management in wilderness: A state-of-knowledge review." In D. Cole and others, eds. *Proceedings: Wilderness science in a time of change, 1999; Vol. 5: Wilderness ecosystems, threats, and management,* 23–48; Missoula, MT. Proceedings RMRS-P-15-Vol-5. USDA Forest Service, Rocky Mountain Research Station, Ogden, UT.

———. 2004. "Managing impacts of campsites." In Ralf Buckley, ed. *Environmental Impact of Tourism.* CABI Publishing, Cambridge, MA. 245–58.

Marion, Jeffrey. 1998. "Recreation ecology research findings: Implications for wilderness and park managers." In "Proceedings of the National Outdoor Ethics Conference, April 18–21, 1996, St. Louis, MO." Izaak Walton League of America, Gaithersburg, MD. 188–96.

———. 2003. "Camping impact management on the Appalachian National Scenic Trail. Appendix 2: Camping Management Practices." Report published by the Appalachian Trail Conference, Harpers Ferry, WV.

Marion, Jeffrey, and David Cole. 1996. "Spatial and temporal variation in soil and vegetation impacts on campsites: Delaware Water Gap National Recreation Area." *Ecological Applications* 6(2):520–30.

Marion, Jeffrey, and Tracy Farrell. 2002. "Management practices that concentrate visitor activities: Camping impact management at Isle Royale National Park, USA." *Journal of Environmental Management* 66(2):201–12.

Marion, Jeffrey, and Jeremy Wimpey. 2007. "Environmental impacts of mountain biking: Science review and best practices." In *Managing Mountain Biking.* Pete Webber, ed. International Mountain Biking Association, Boulder, CO. 94–111.

McClaran, Mitchel, and David Cole. 1993. "Packstock in wilderness: Use, impacts, monitoring, and management." Gen. Tech. Rpt. INT-301. USDA Forest Service, Intermountain Research Station, Ogden, UT.

Pickering, Catherine, Wendy Hill, David Newsome, and Yu-Fai Leung. 2010. "Comparing hiking, mountain biking and horse riding impacts on vegetation and soils in Australia and the United States of America." *Journal of Environmental Management* 91:551–62.

Spildie, David, David Cole, and Sarah Walker. 2000. "Effectiveness of a confinement strategy in reducing pack stock impacts at campsites in the Selway-Bitterroot Wilderness, Idaho." In D. Cole and others, eds. *Proceedings: Wilderness science in a time of change, 1999; Vol. 5: Wilderness ecosystems, threats, and management,* 199–208; Missoula, MT. Proceedings RMRS-P-15-Vol-5. USDA Forest Service, Rocky Mountain Research Station, Ogden, UT.

Tread Lightly. 2012. Tread Lightly 101 Online Awareness Course. (www .treadlightly.org)

Wimpey, Jeremy, and Jeffrey Marion. 2010. "The influence of use, environmental and managerial factors on the width of recreational trails." *Journal of Environmental Management* 91:2028–37.

Dispose of Waste Properly

Bridle, Kerry, and Jamie Kirkpatrick. 2003. "Impacts of nutrient additions and digging for human waste disposal in natural environments, Tasmania, Australia." *Journal of Environmental Management* 69(3):299–306.

———. 2005. "An analysis of the breakdown of paper products (toilet paper, tissues and tampons) in natural environments, Tasmania, Australia." *Journal of Environmental Management* 74:21–30.

Campbell, Jonathan, and David Gibson. 2001. "The effect of seeds of exotic species transported via horse dung on vegetation along trail corridors." *Plant Ecology* 157:23–35.

Cilimburg, Amy, Christopher Monz, and Sharon Kehoe. 2000. "Wildlife recreation and human waste: A review of problems, practices, and concerns." *Environmental Management* 25(6):587–98.

Civil, Karen, and Brett McNamara. 2000. Best practice human waste management workshop. Workshop proceedings, Canberra & Jindabyne, Australian Alps Liaison Committee, Environment Australia.

Clow, David, Rachael Peavler, Jim Roche, Anna Panorska, James Thomas, and Steve Smith. 2011. "Assessing possible visitor-use impacts on water quality in Yosemite National Park." *California. Environmental Monitoring and Assessment* 183:197–215.

Derlet, Robert, K. Ger, John Richards, and James Carlson. 2008. "Risk factors for coliform bacteria in backcountry lakes and streams in the Sierra Nevada Mountains: A 5-Year study." *Wilderness & Environmental Medicine* 19:82–90.

Ells, Michael, and Christopher Monz. 2011. "The consequences of backcountry surface disposal of human waste in an alpine, temperate forest and arid environment." *Journal of Environmental Management* 92(4):1334–37.

Hargreaves, Joanna. 2006. "Laboratory evaluation of the 3-bowl system used for washing-up eating utensils in the field." *Wilderness & Environmental Medicine* 17:94–102.

Ketcham, Peter. 2001. "Backcountry sanitation manual." Green Mountain Club and the Appalachian Trail Conservancy, Harpers Ferry, WV.

Lachapelle, Paul. "Sanitation in wilderness: Balancing minimum tool policies and wilderness values." In D. Cole and others, eds. *Proceedings: Wilderness science in a time of change, 1999; Vol. 5: Wilderness ecosystems, threats, and management,* 141–47; Missoula, MT. Proceedings RMRS-P-15-Vol-5. USDA Forest Service, Rocky Mountain Research Station, Ogden, UT.

Land, Brenda. 1995. "Remote waste management." USDA Forest Service, Technology & Development Program, Report 9523-1202-SDTDC.

Lenth, Benjamin, Mark Brennan, and Richard Knight. 2006. "The effects of dogs on wildlife communities." Research report to City of Boulder Open Space and Mountain Parks. Boulder, CO.

Meyer, Kathleen. 1994. *How to Shit in the Woods.* 2nd ed. Ten Speed Press, Berkeley, CA.

Temple, Kenneth, Anne Camper, and Gordon McFeters. 1980. "Survival of two Enterobacteria in feces buried in soil under field conditions." *Applied & Environmental Microbiology* 40(4):794–97.

Temple, Kenneth, Anne Camper, and Robert Lucas. 1982. "Potential health hazard from human wastes in wilderness." *Journal of Soil & Water Conservation* 37(6):357–59.

Wells, F., and W. Laurenroth. 2007. "The potential for horses to disperse alien plants along recreational trails." *Rangeland Ecology & Management* 60:574–77.

Wilkinson, Donald, Daniel Armstrong, and Dale Blevins. 2002. "Effects of wastewater and combined sewer overflows on water quality in the Blue River Basin, Kansas City, Missouri and Kansas, July 1998–October 2000." U.S. Geological Survey, Water-Resources Investigations Report 02–4107.

Leave What You Find

Belzer, Bill, and Mary Steisslinger. 1999. "The box turtle: Room with a view on species decline." *The American Biology Teacher* 61(7):510–13.

DiVittorio, Joe, Michael Grodowitz, and Joe Snow. 2010. "Inspection and cleaning manual for Equipment and vehicles to prevent the spread of invasive species. Technical Memorandum No. 86-68220-07-05. USDI Bureau of Reclamation, Denver, CO.

Gower, Stith. 2008. "Are horses responsible for introducing non-native plants along forest trails in the eastern United States?" *Forest Ecology & Management* 256:997–1003.

Humane Society of the United States. 2009. "Should wild animals be kept as pets?" Washington, DC.

McLeod, Lianne. 2012. "Wild animals as pets: Ethical issues and potential pitfalls." http://exoticpets.about.com/od/exoticpetsissues/a/wildanimals.htm. Accessed: Jan. 8, 2014.

Mount, Ann, and Catherine Pickering. 2009. "Testing the capacity of clothing to act as a vector for non-native seed in protected areas." *Journal of Environmental Management* 91:168–79.

Partners in Amphibian and Reptile Conservation. 2012. "Please don't turn it loose." www.parcplace.org. Pamphlet. Arizona Game & Fish Department, Phoenix, AZ.

Pickering, Catherine, and Ann Mount. 2010. "Do tourists disperse weed seed? A global review of unintentional human-mediated terrestrial seed dispersal on clothing, vehicles and horses." *Journal of Sustainable Tourism* 18(2):239–56.

Potito, Aaron, and Susan Beatty. 2005. "Impacts of recreation trails on exotic and ruderal species distribution in grassland areas along the Colorado Front Range." *Environmental Management* 36(2):230–36.

Prinbeck, Gwenn, Denise Lach, and Samuel Chan. 2009. "Exploring stakehold-ers' attitudes and beliefs regarding behaviors that prevent the spread of inva-sive species." *Environmental Education Research* 17(3):341–52.

Root, Samantha, and Catherine O'Reilly. 2012. "Didymo control: Increasing the effectiveness of decontamination strategies and reducing spread." *Fisheries* 37(10):440–48.

Schuppli, C., and D. Fraser. 2000. "A framework for assessing the suitability of different species as companion animals." *Animal Welfare* 9:259–372.

Ward, Caroline, and Joseph Roggenbuck. 2003. "Understanding park visitors' responses to interventions to reduce petrified wood theft." *Journal of Interpre-tation Research* 8(1):67–82.

Western Regional Panel on Aquatic Nuisance Species. 2009. "Quagga-zebra mus-sel action plan for western U.S. waters." Aquatic Nuisance Species Task Force.

Wildesen, Leslie. 1982. "The study of impacts to archaeological sites." *Advances in Archaeological Method & Theory* 5:51–96.

Wisconsin Council on Forestry. 2008. "Best management practices for preventing the spread of invasive species by outdoor recreation activities in Wisconsin."

Wittenberg, Rudiger, and Matthew Cock, eds. 2001. "Invasive alien species: A toolkit of best prevention and management practices." Global Invasive Species Programme. CAB International, Wallingford, UK.

Minimize Campfire Impacts

Bull, Evelyn. 2002. "The value of coarse woody debris to vertebrates in the Pacific Northwest." Gen. Tech. Rpt. PSW-GTR-181. USDA Forest Service, Pacific Northwest Research Station, LaGrande, OR.

Bratton, Susan, and Linda Stromberg. 1982. "Firewood gathering impacts in backcountry campsites in Great Smoky Mountains National Park." *Environ-mental Management* 6(1):63–71.

Christensen, Neal, and David Cole. 2000. "Leave No Trace practices: behaviors and preferences of wilderness visitors regarding use of cookstoves and camp-ing away from lakes." In D. Cole and others, eds. *Proceedings: Wilderness sci-ence in a time of change, 1999; Vol. 5: Wilderness ecosystems, threats, and management,* 77–85; Missoula, MT. Proceedings RMRS-P-15-Vol-5. USDA Forest Service, Rocky Mountain Research Station, Ogden, UT.

Cole, David. 1995. "Rationale behind fire building and wood gathering prac-tices." Master Network, Leave No Trace Newsletter 7:12–13.

Cole, David N., and John Dalle-Molle. 1982. "Managing campfire impacts in the backcountry." General Tech. Rpt. INT-135, USDA Forest Service, Intermoun-tain Forest & Range Experiment Station, Ogden, UT.

Davies, Mary. 2004. "What's burning in your campfire? Garbage in, toxics out." USDA Forest Service, Technology & Development Program, Rpt. 0423-2327-MTDC, Missoula, MT.

Fenn, Dennis, Jay Gogue, and Raymond Burge. 1976. "Effects of campfires on soil properties." Ecological Services Bulletin 76-20782. USDI National Park Serv-ice, Washington, D.C.

Hall, T. E., and T. A. Farrell. 2001. "Fuelwood depletion at wilderness campsites: Extent and potential ecological significance." *Environmental Conservation* 28:1–7.

Hammitt, William E. 1982. "Alternatives to banning campfires." *Parks* 7, 3:8–9.

———. 1980. "Fire rings in the backcountry: Are they necessary?" *Parks* 5:8–9.

Houck, James, Andrew Scott, Jared Sorenson, and Bruce Davis. 2000. "Comparison of air emissions between cordwood and wax-sawdust firelogs burned in residential fireplaces." In *Proceedings of AWMA & PNIS international specialty conference: Recent advances in the science of management of air toxics, Banff, Alberta.*

Jacobi, W., B. Goodrich, and C. Cleaver. 2011. "Firewood transport by National and State Park campers: A risk for native or exotic tree pest movement." *Arboriculture & Urban Forestry* 37(3):126–38.

Marion, Jeffrey. 2003. "Camping impact management on the Appalachian National Scenic Trail. Appendix 2: Camping Management Practices." Report published by the Appalachian Trail Conference, Harpers Ferry, WV.

Reid, Scott, and Jeffrey Marion. 2005. "A comparison of campfire impacts and policies in seven protected areas." *Environmental Management* 36(1):48–58.

Trickel, Robert, Nicole Wulff, and Bill Jones. 2012. "Invasive species and firewood movement." Fact Sheet 5.4, Don't Move Firewood website: www.dontmovefirewood.org.

Vachowski, Brian. 1997. "Leave No Trace campfires and firepans." USDA Forest Service, Technology & Development Program. Rpt. 9723-2815-MTDC, Missoula, MT.

Respect Wildlife

Anderson, S. H. 1995. "Recreational disturbance and wildlife populations." *Wildlife and recreation: Coexistence through management and research.* Island Press, Washington, DC.

Cole, David, and Richard Knight. 1991. "Wildlife preservation and recreational use: Conflicting goals of wildland management." In *Transactions of the 56th North American Wildlife & Natural Resources Conference.* 233–37.

Cole, David, and Peter Landres. 1995. "Indirect effects of recreationists on wildlife." In R. Knight and K. Gutzwiller, eds. *Wildlife and recreationists: co-existence through management and research.* Island Press, Washington, DC.

Coleman, John, and Stanley Temple. 1993. "Rural residents' free-ranging domestic cats: A survey." *Wildlife Society Bulletin* 21: 381–90.

Coleman, John, Stanley Temple, and Scott Craven. 1997. "Cats and wildlife: A conservation dilemma." Texas Parks & Wildlife, Austin, TX.

Dahlgren, R., and C. Korschgen. 1992. "Human disturbances of waterfowl: An annotated bibliography." Rpt. 188, U.S. Fish & Wildlife Service, Washington, DC.

Garber, Steven, and Joanna Burger. 1995. "A 20-yr study documenting the relationship between turtle decline and human recreation." *Ecological Applications* 5(4):1151–62.

Gookin, J., and T. Reed. 2009. *NOLS bear essentials: Hiking and camping in bear country.* Stackpole Books, Mechanicsburg, PA.

Gutzwiller, Kevin. 1995. "Recreational disturbance and wildlife communities." In R. Knight and K. Gutzwiller, eds. *Wildlife and recreationists: Coexistence through management and research.* Island Press, Washington, DC.

Hartley, William. 1996. *Loving nature . . . the right way: A family guide to viewing and photographing scenic areas and wildlife.* IntroNet Solutions, Inc., Minneapolis, MN.

Joslin, G., and H. Youmans (coordinators). 1999. "Effects of recreation on Rocky Mountain wildlife: A review for Montana." Committee on Effects of Recreation on Wildlife, Montana Chapter of The Wildlife Society.

Knight, Richard, and David Cole. 1991. "Effects of recreational activity on wildlife in wildlands." Transactions of the 56th North American Wildlife & Natural Resources Conference. 238–46.

Knight, R. L., S. A. Temple. 1995. "Wildlife and recreationists: Co-existence through management." Chapter 20 in R. L. Knight and K. J. Gutzwiller, eds. *Wildlife and recreationists: Coexistence through management and research.* Island Press, Washington, DC.

Lindsay, Karen, John Craig, and Matthew Low. 2008. "Tourism and conservation: The effects of track proximity on avian reproductive success and nest selection in an open sanctuary." *Tourism Management* 29:730–39.

Loss, S. R., T. Will, and P. P. Marra. 2013. "The impact of free-ranging domestic cats on wildlife of the United States." *Nature Communications* 4: 1396 doi: 10.1038/ncomms2380.

Marion, Jeffrey, Robert Dvorak, and Robert Manning. 2008. "Wildlife feeding in parks: Methods for monitoring the effectiveness of educational interventions and wildlife food attraction behaviors." *Human Dimensions of Wildlife* 13:429–42

Orams, Mark. 2002. "Feeding wildlife as a tourism attraction: A review of issues and impacts." *Tourism Management* 23:281–93.

Rogers, Lynn. 1991. "Reactions of black bears to human menstrual odors." *Journal of Wildlife Management* 55(4):632–34.

Smith, T., S. Herrero, T. DeBruyn, and J. Wilder. 2008. "Efficacy of bear deterrent spray in Alaska." *The Journal of Wildlife Management* 72(3):640–45.

Taylor, Ken, Ros Taylor, Kath Longden, and Paul Fisher. 2005. "Dogs, access and nature conservation." English Nature Rpt 649. Peterborough, England.

Vachowski, Brian. 1994. "Low impact food hoists." USDA Forest Service. 9523-2809-MTDC.

Be Considerate of Other Visitors

Manning, Robert. 2007. *Parks and carrying capacity: Commons without tragedy.* Island Press, Washington, DC.

Manning, Robert, and Laura Anderson. 2012. *Managing outdoor recreation: Case studies in the national parks.* CABI, Cambridge, MA.

Pilcher, Ericka, Peter Newman, and Robert Manning. 2009. "Understanding and managing experiential aspects of soundscapes at Muir Woods National Monument." *Environmental Management* 43:425–35.

Schneider, Ingrid. 2000. "Revisiting and revising recreation conflict research." *Journal of Leisure Research* 32(1):129–32.

Stewart, William P., David N. Cole. 2001. "Number of encounters and experience quality in Grand Canyon backcountry; consistently negative and weak relationships." *Journal of Leisure Research* 33(1): 106–20.

Watson, Alan, Daniel Williams, and John Daigle. 1991. "Sources of conflict between hikers and mountain bike riders in the Rattlesnake NRA." *Journal of Park & Recreation Administration* 9(3):59–71.

Leave No Trace Ethics

Ajzen, I. 2002. "Perceived behavioral control, self-efficacy, locus of control, and the theory of planned behavior." *Journal of Applied Social Psychology* 32(4):665–83.

Bromley, Maria, Jeffrey Marion, and Troy Hall. 2013. "Training to teach Leave No Trace: Efficacy of Master Educator courses." *Journal of Park and Recreation Administration*. 31(4): 62–78.

Daniels, Melissa, and Jeffrey Marion. 2006. "Communicating Leave No Trace ethics and practices: Efficacy of two-day Trainer Courses." *Journal of Park & Recreation Administration* 23(4):1–19.

D'Antonio, Ashley, Christopher Monz, Peter Newman, and others. 2012. "The effects of local ecological knowledge, minimum-impact knowledge, and prior experience on visitor perceptions of the ecological impacts of backcountry recreation." *Environmental Management* 50:542–54.

Douchette, Joseph, and David Cole. 1993. "Wilderness visitor education: Information about alternative techniques." Gen. Tech. Rpt. INT-295, USDA Forest Service, Intermountain Research Station, Ogden, UT.

Fishbein, M., and M. Manfredo. 1992. "A theory of behavior change." In M. Manfredo, ed. *Influencing human behavior: Theory and application in recreation, tourism, and natural resources management.* 29–50. Sagamore Publishing Inc., Champaign, IL.

Ham, Sam, Terry Brown, Jim Curtis, and others. 2007. "Promoting persuasion in protected areas: A guide for managers." Sustainable Tourism CRC, Strategic Communication and Visitor Behaviour, Gold Coast, Australia.

Harding, James, William Borrie, and David Cole. 2000. "Factors that limit compliance with low-impact recommendations." In D. Cole and others, eds. *Proceedings: Wilderness science in a time of change, 1999; Vol 4: Wilderness visitors, experiences, and visitor management,* 198–202; Missoula, MT. Proceedings RMRS-P-15-VOL-4. USDA Forest Service, Rocky Mountain Research Station, Ogden, UT.

Manning, Robert. 2011. *Studies in outdoor recreation: Search and research for satisfaction.* 3rd ed. Oregon State University Press, Corvallis, OR.

Marion, Jeffrey, Ben Lawhon, Wade Vagias, and Peter Newman. 2011. "Revisiting 'Beyond Leave No Trace.'" *Ethics, Place & Environment* 14(2):231–37.
Marion, Jeffrey, and Scott Reid. 2007. "Minimising visitor impacts to protected areas: The efficacy of low impact education programmes." *Journal of Sustainable Tourism* 15(1): 5–27.
Oelschlaeger, Max. 1995. "Taking the land ethic outdoors: its implications for recreation." In R. Knight and K. Gutzwiller, eds. 335–50. *Wildlife and Recreationists: Coexistence through Management and Research*. Island Press, Washington, DC.
Simon, Gregory, and Peter Alagona. 2009. "Beyond Leave No Trace." *Ethics, Place & Environment* 12(1):17–34.
Vagias, Wade, and Robert Powell. 2010. "Backcountry visitors' Leave No Trace attitudes." *International Journal of Wilderness* 16(3):21–27.

A Brief History of the Leave No Trace Program

Hampton, Bruce, and David Cole. *Soft Paths: How to Use the Wilderness Without Harming It*. Stackpole Books, Mechanicsburg, PA.
Hart, John. 1977. *Walking softly in the wilderness: The Sierra Club guide to backpacking*. Sierra Club Books, San Francisco, CA.
Marion, Jeffrey, and Scott Reid. 2001. "Development of the United States Leave No Trace program: A historical perspective." In M. Usher, ed. *Enjoyment and Understanding of the Natural Heritage*. Scottish Natural Heritage, Edinburgh, The Stationery Office Ltd., Scotland. 81–92.
Petzoldt, Paul. 1974. *The Wilderness Handbook*. W.W. Norton & Co., New York.
Waterman, Laura and Guy. 1979. *Backwoods ethics: Environmental concerns for hikers and campers*.

Links to Research

Aldo Leopold Wilderness Research Institute: www.leopold.wilderness.net
Arthur Carhart National Wilderness Training Center: www.carhart.wilderness.net
Leave No Trace Research: www.LNT.org/teach/research
Outdoor Education Research and Evaluation Center: www.wilderdom.com/research.html
Outdoor Industry Association: www.outdoorindustry.org
Recreation Ecology Research Network: www.cnr.ncsu.edu/rern
Wilderness.net: www.wilderness.net

Author Biography

Jeffrey L. Marion, PhD, grew up exploring the woods, streams, and caves of Kentucky. Introduced to outdoor activities through Scouting, he developed a passion for nature and high-adventure outdoor activities. He combined his outdoor interests with academic studies through graduate research in recreation ecology—a field of study that examines the environmental impacts of visitation on protected natural areas. Hired as a scientist by the National Park Service in 1985, he has conducted visitor impact studies and consultations in dozens of U.S. and international parks. The aim of this research is to develop practices that avoid or minimize visitor impacts from hiking, camping, climbing, and other outdoor activities. Transferred to the U.S. Geological Survey in 1997, Marion expanded his recreation ecology research to include national forests, wildlife preserves, and other natural areas.

Dr. Marion was a founding member of the Board of Directors of Leave No Trace beginning in 1994, and chaired the Educational Review Committee for a decade, during which time he helped plan and develop the Leave No Trace principles, outdoor practices, educational materials, and courses. He has also assisted the Boy Scouts of America in incorporating Leave No Trace throughout their publications and programs. An active outdoorsman, he has shared his passion for outdoor activities by serving for over a dozen years first as a Scoutmaster and then as leader of a co-ed Venture Crew active in high-adventure outings.

Dr. Marion is employed by the U.S. Geological Survey and stationed at Virginia Tech in Blacksburg, where he also serves as an adjunct professor in the College of Natural Resources and Environment.

Acknowledgments

The low-impact outdoor practices presented in these pages have been developed and refined over decades and will continue to evolve in the future. Many originated in the early federal agency minimum impact pamphlets of the 1970s focusing on wilderness. These evolved into a more formal interagency "No-Trace" program in the 1980s and a partnership with the National Outdoor Leadership School in the 1990s to develop more comprehensive practices, literature, and courses.

The Leave No Trace Center for Outdoor Ethics Educational Review Committee became responsible for developing and refining low-impact practices beginning in 1997, including a revision of principles in 1999, development of the Frontcountry program in 2002, and continuing development of low-impact practices for different recreational activities and environments. I acknowledge the substantial contributions made to the Leave No Trace educational messaging made by this committee, which I chaired until 2005 and have been serving as a member of thereafter. The committee's membership has included representatives from the U.S. Forest Service, National Park Service, Bureau of Land Management, National Outdoor Leadership School, Outward Bound, Appalachian Mountain Club, Boy Scouts of America, and several other organizations. All have contributed substantially in developing, refining, and approving the low-impact practices included in this book.

My thanks and gratitude for the assistance and careful reviews performed by several agencies and organizations, particularly the National Park Service, U.S. Forest Service, Bureau of Land Management, U.S. Geological Survey, Leave No Trace Center for Outdoor Ethics, National Outdoor Leadership School, Boy Scouts of America, and Appalachian Trail

Conservancy. The following individuals contributed helpful reviews: Ben Lawhon, Tom Banks, Charlie Thorpe, Dan Howells, Dave Bates, Rich Brame, Andy Downs, Toby Green, Bruce Hanat, Howard Kern, Patti Klein, Yu-Fai Leung, Rhonda Mickelson, and Howard Kern.

Leave No Trace Promoting Environmental Awareness in Kids (PEAK)

The PEAK program is designed to educate children about the outdoors and the responsible use of our shared public lands. It is based on the seven principles of Leave No Trace. The PEAK Pack includes six fun activities designed especially for kids. PEAK is ideal for the elementary school age group. Each activity or "module" can be delivered in 30–60 minutes depending on group size and available time. The modules come in durable plastic folders that can be used in the field or in a classroom setting. Also available in Spanish!

Purchase packs here: LNT.org/shop/product/peak-pack